Straight Talk.........

THRIVING
in BUSINESS

the **publishing** CIRCLE

STRAIGHT TALK: THRIVING IN BUSINESS / DANNY CREED
ISBN 978-1-947398-46-7   (PAPERBACK)
ISBN 978-1-947398-63-4   (LARGE-PRINT PAPERBACK)
ISBN 978-1-947398-56-6   (HARDBACK)
ISBN 978-1-947398-58-0   (EBOOK)

Book design by Michele Uplinger

Straight Talk.........

THRIVING
in BUSINESS

DANNY **CREED**

People are talking about

Straight Talk........

ON THRIVING IN BUSINESS
by Danny Creed

"I have had the privilege of working with Coach Dan on several projects and always found his candor and tenacity refreshing. I have also found his insights and advice extremely valuable. This book is all that and more. If you are an entrepreneur or thinking of becoming one, this is a must-read. Learning how to be honest with yourself and how to do some important "critical thinking" will save you time, grief, and possibly a fortune. Dan's no BS approach to business and life is a formula for success and the sooner you adopt the winning attitude he teaches in his latest book, the faster you will achieve success in business and life."

NICK MARINIELLO
PRESIDENT OF UPSTREAM BUSINESS CONSULTING
& TRUSTED ADVISOR TO AMBITIOUS ENTREPRENEURS

• • •

"*Straight Talk . . . Thriving in Business* is a five-star read. Danny's no nonsense, down-to-earth approach puts the whole business question in a refreshing light. You won't be able to put it down!"

CARL HUGHES
EXECUTIVE DIRECTOR
BROTHERS IN BLUE REENTRY, INC.

"Danny shows once again why he is considered *the* Coach to Coaches."

CHRIS CEBOLLERO
BEST-SELLING AUTHOR OF *Ultimate Success*

•   •   •

"This book by Dan Creed is spot on, providing no-nonsense advice to be successful in business today. I have had the pleasure of working with Dan on opportunities and as a business coach. What really stands out to me in this book is the way Dan gives it to you straight. No sugar coating it: success takes clarity, purpose, passion, planning, sales savvy and the need to outwork your competitors every day. I can always spot theoretical or book-smart writers who have never had to deliver the goods. Take it from me, everything Dan delivers in this book is rock-solid advice from someone who has absolutely had to practice what he preaches. A real 'must read' for experienced and new leaders alike on just what it takes to be great, written by the greatest Business Coach I have ever encountered in my career."

GLENN MILLER
VICE PRESIDENT
BUSINESS SOLUTIONS, AMERICAN SOLUTIONS FOR BUSINESS

•   •   •

"*Straight Talk . . . Thriving in Business* is 'must-read, dead-serious, essential insight' for having a successful business. Don't read at your own peril."

FRANK AGIN
FOUNDER & PRESIDENT
AMSPIRIT BUSINESS CONNECTIONS

•   •   •

"Danny Creed is the brightest star in the universe of personal and business development in the 21st century. A dominant force in the world of personal and business success, he provides the little-known secrets, priceless inspiration, and real-world strategies necessary to reach the heights of success in life and business. As a business advisor and author, there are few sources I trust to provide me with the solutions I need to continue thriving on personal and professional levels. Among my most trusted sources is Danny Creed. If you want to win the game of life and business, you'll discover the edge you need in *Straight Talk* on Business!"

JOHN ECHOLS
PRESIDENT of MINDBIZ COACHING & CONSULTING, INC.
AUTHOR of *The Peak Power Formula*

• • •

"In his new book, *Straight Talk . . . Thriving in Business*, Coach Dan has distilled years of wisdom and knowledge that have contributed to his success into practical, organized, easy-to-understand language. Every page is packed with useful tips and actionable steps, so you will want to keep this close at hand for a reference. It's also a fun read, and you will get new ideas every time you pick it up. If you have the discipline to follow the processes clearly detailed here, you will be more successful in business and more successful in life. Thanks to Coach Dan for his willingness to share his 'secrets' for *Thriving in Business*."

CARL ANDERSON
BUSINESS OWNER

• • •

"I've been following Coach Danny Creed for quite a while and the content in his latest book is accelerating my business knowledge exponentially. It's straight talk, written without fluff, and he gets to the core of each subject quickly. Coach tells it like it is in the business world, and he speaks with authority because he is the 'real deal.' I highly recommend *Straight Talk . . . Thriving in Business* to any professional who is looking for the tools necessary to succeed 10x in business and in life."

KAREN ROANE
FOUNDER of NEW DESTINY MARKETING, LLC

"There is wisdom and timeless business advice inside *Thriving in Business*. I have read a lot of books on business, beginning with Dale Carnegie's *How to Win Friends and Influence People*. The best books were written by people with holes in their shoes from beating the street to make sales or with dirty fingernails from working a business from the bottom up.

Danny Creed's experience, power of observation, and integration gives you a dose of real-world walking-around sense that is not based on AI, big spreadsheets, or Ivy League diplomas. His book teaches anyone—from a teenager to a business mogul—how to improve your skills and get smart quick about the foundations of business success. Readers take away a practical understanding of how to put that knowledge to work.

Dan explains that business is about more than business—it's about life. It's about balance, not deluding yourself, and about understanding people. He'll help you see that to become a real leader—that is, someone who's employees say is one—you must serve more than mammon. True leadership is helping others achieve greater things than they thought possible, inspiring and giving them hope and a vision of creating a future that could change the world. Steve Jobs, Elon Musk, Jack Kennedy, and others have changed our very world with inspiring and uplifting goals we believe in. What people are inspired to believe they can achieve, they will . . . or darn near die trying.

If you have a son, daughter, or grandchild, give them this book. Tell them, 'If you read this book, think about it deeply, and apply what it teaches, you'll gain a business education you can't buy at Harvard or achieve on your own. Because of this book, when you enter the workforce, your knowledge of how the real business world works will shoot you past others like a bottle rocket on the 4th of July.

This book provides the insights any businessperson needs to meet any challenges they face. "

CHRIS DEKLE
BUSINESS CONSULTING / COACHING & MARKETING SERVICES

"Forget about all the other books about business success. This is the only one you need. The recipe is here, all you need to add is the effort."

MICHAEL R. MARTENS
MANAGING PARTNER
FIRST STAFF BENEFITS LLC

• • •

"Don't make a major business move until you read Straight Talk on Business. This book will walk you and your business through the basics and put you on the right track to boldly move forward. Roll up your sleeves and do a few warmup exercises before sitting down with *Straight Talk . . . Thriving in Business*. And, don't miss the 40% Rule on page 75."

MARC MCCOY
AUTHOR of
The Time of My Life Began When the Doctor Numbered My Days

"This cover-it-all business book of the future is Danny Creed's *Straight Talk . . . Thriving in Business*. Whether you read it cover-to-cover or pick it up and randomly pick a new page each day, it's impossible to not be a better businessperson after this book."

TYLER ROBINSON
R.O.C.K. CONSULTING

• • •

"Coach Dan shares powerful insights into the entrepreneurial business world that, if used, will launch your business into a successful future."

MIKE MELCHER
R.O.C.K. CONSULTING

• • •

"This life-and-business tutorial offers everything an entrepreneur will ever need to build self-confidence so strong that you will be able to rise the top, reach the highest goals, be ready in all situations, and beat all obstacles much easier than you think."

MISKO KRSMANOVIC
BUSINESSMAN & ENTREPRENEUR
BELGRADE, SERBIA

• • •

"You're good at what you do—how do you keep your knife sharp? This book is the sharpening stone for your business knife. It walks you back through the fundamentals you had to learn to get here, then hones you for the future against time-proven insights on how the good get better and stay sharp. If you've ever wished you had kept for quick reference all the lessons you learned on your first climb to success, you'll love *Straight Talk . . . Thriving in Business*. Perfect for your business' leadership team and anybody else whose future success you care about."

JACK HOSTERMAN
EXECUTIVE SENIOR PARTNER, MILITARY DIVISION
LUCAS GROUP

"In an age of hyper-specialization, it's increasingly rare to find someone who seems to have 'the whole picture' when it comes to business. Danny Creed is one of those rare folks.

We're inundated with books filled with hundreds of pages and nothing practical to tell us. At best, we might obtain some insight into a single topic. With *Straight Talk . . . Thriving in Business* we're presented with chapter after chapter of actionable strategies and tactics based in real-world experience, not only through building businesses of his own, but in coaching tens of thousands of other entrepreneurs, C-suite executives, and owners. No matter where you are in your business, or where you struggle most, you'll find the answers in this book. Of course, you still have to do the work!"

BRYCE KUHLMAN
CEO of THE HOLISEC GROUP

"Coach Dan's book, *Straight Talk . . . Thriving in Business* is a must read for ANYONE working in the business world. It's the same great content you get when working personally with Coach and when applied, can change your business drastically. I highly recommend this book to anyone wanting to move into an entirely new level of business mastery."

JESSICA ADNANI
FOUNDER & CEO
PERSONALIZED SOLUTIONS & PODCAST PHX

• • •

"So much wonderful and practical advice in here. It's straight to the point, without all the extra clutter I find in most books on business and career. Some real gems in there!"

GREG HELLER
CEO of VIDEO IMPACT MARKETING
BURBANK CALIFORNIA

"*Straight Talk . . . Thriving in Business* is an enjoyable and indispensable book for busy leaders who don't have time or patience for fluff. Dan's no-nonsense, straight-talk approach cuts through the BS and jargon and gets right to the point—helping you win. Every page has proven, actionable strategies to grow your business to the next level."

BRANDON DOW
COO of ORION HOMES
ARIZONA'S #1 BEHAVIORAL HEALTH RESIDENTIAL PROVIDER

• • •

"As a coach, clarity is the most important ingredient in the recipe for success. If you want clarity as a coach, you ask questions. If you want clarity in your life, pick up Danny Creed's book *A Life Best Lived* and read EVERY PAGE."

MIKE MELCHER & TYLER ROBINSON
R.O.C.K. CONSULTING

"This is a must read for any business owner—invest in yourself, invest in your business, and invest in your employees."

STEVE MURPHY
CEO of MURPHY & COMPANY, LLC

"*Straight Talk . . . Thriving in Business* isn't your typical book on business. You can tell the author has rolled up his sleeves and done the work. This book should be any entrepreneur's encyclopedia on how to start, scale, and maintain your business. The techniques and concepts in this book are how I have taken my company to over $50 million in premium in just one year."

ERIC SANCHEZ
CEO of EMPLOYEE RETENTION BENEFITS, LOS ANGELES, CALIFORNIA

• • •

"My friend and mentor, Danny Creed, has done it again. Danny takes the complexity of thriving in business, which can be overwhelming, and distills it to principles that lead to action. As always, Danny provides intuitive action steps that will make you a better entrepreneur, employee, and person. Thanks again, Danny."

STEVE RADLEY
PRESIDENT & CEO
KANSAS CENTER FOR ENTREPRENEURSHIP

• • •

"This book is for those people who have read a hundred business books but need a cheat sheet to help them answer a current question, make important decisions, and take the next steps in their business development. I know Danny Creed personally and professionally, and if I were going to start a business (or go to war), Danny would be one of the few people I'd want on my team. Everything in this book is pragmatic, in-your-face, and super valuable. *Don't* read it at your peril."

BROTHER CRAIG MARSHALL
DIRECTOR OF EDUCATION of MONK IN A BOX

CONTENTS ...

• • •

To all my mentors in this entrepreneurial journey. Some are famous, others are not. They may be people you've never heard of who have, for whatever cosmic reason, found me in my life journey and shared their wisdom, or precisely and strategically kicked my butt when it most needed to be kicked. Many have passed on, but all helped to mold and change my life. The lessons they've shared are ones I think about every day, and more than likely will continue to think about, until that day I move on. Until that day comes, I will always be eternally grateful for their time, patience, friendship, and love!

• • •

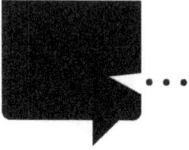

A man went to his bank manager and said, "I'd like to start a small business. How do I go about it?

"Simple," said the bank manager. "Buy a big business and then wait!"

• • •

"If you're trying to achieve, there will be roadblocks. I've had them; everybody has had them. But obstacles don't have to stop you. If you run into a wall, don't turn around and give up. Figure out how to climb it, go through it, or work around it"

MICHAEL JORDAN

• • •

When a business manager was fired, not only did he have to give back his company credit card and his company car, he even had to give back his ulcer.

Did you hear about the guy who trained in origami and opened a shop in the local mall? The business folded.

● ● ●

"We find no real satisfaction or happiness in life without obstacles to conquer and goals to achieve."

MAXWELL MALTZ

● ● ●

A chicken and a pig were drinking in a bar one night when the chicken said: "Why don't we go into business together? We could open a ham and egg restaurant."

"Not so fast," said the pig. "For you, it's just a day's work. For me, it's a matter of life and death."

Foreword

I am a lucky man.

You've heard people say that before, I'm sure. But have you noticed there's "just something" about lucky people?

What is it? Is the universe just smiling at them more? Are they simply in the right place at the right time?

For me, my luck seems to be specific. And I should add that most of the time, I don't feel lucky at all. I rarely gamble or take big risks.

So, why would I say something so bold as "I am a lucky man?"

It's because I've had the good fortune to meet and work with terrific people all over the world. I'm lucky because I get to work with compelling, inspiring, no BS, straight shooters who are here to change the world.

In 2008, I got lucky.

I met a man who was both charismatic and humble, friendly and fierce, and who had that rare ability to move between being a teacher and student with ease. Plus, he could play the harmonica!

Let me back up, because before you read this book, I think you'll appreciate some context. I am an entrepreneur. This might sound strange to you, but it took me many years to feel comfortable saying that.

As I look back over my career, one covering real estate, mail-order, online retail pharmacy, call centers, professional services franchising, and business coaching, it turns out I haven't had a real job in almost twenty-five years! I'm even less employable now. So, really, I need to be okay saying I'm a serial entrepreneur. And I am.

About fifteen years ago, I bought a small professional services company that was franchising business coaching using the brand, systems, and processes of the famous author and business guru, Brian Tracy.

Again, I felt like the luckiest man in the world. Not only did I get to meet my mentor and the author of multiple books and how-to strategies I have subsequently put in place—I now found myself in business with him.

In fifteen years, we grew from just six franchisees in the US to over 200 in nine countries. I got lucky again because I got to work with some of the finest people, and we were doing the greatest work. Helping others.

Enter Dan Creed.

In 2008, Dan was part of a monumental training class, consisting of a grand total of two (yes two, that's not a typo) people. And the other guy left the training when his wife had a bizarre accident at home.

So, there I was, a single trainer, working with a single new franchisee. For most people, that would be awkward, but not for us.

I learned that both Dan and I are real-world, no BS, reality-only business improvement guys. We're here to G.S.D. (Get S—T Done) and we love to help others.

I'm fond of saying, "It ain't what you've got, it's what you do with what you've got that's important."

Dan went from being thv only guy left in an underwhelming training class to a consistent record setter in our company. And by record-setting, I mean he dominated by factors of ten.

- He brought on clients and got them fantastic results
- He brought on near-bankrupt clients and turned them into multi-millionaires
- He gleefully pushed the edges of our systems and processes and pulled out better results than ever before
- He became one of our trainers so he could pass on his coaching style and formula for leading and winning on to other great coaches

He holds a special place that has no title, but immense power.

He's an influencer. I can make policy and process, but Dan can change hearts.

If I had to pick a Halloween costume that fit Dan by personality, conviction, action, and impact, I think I'd have him walk out dressed as a knight. A white knight, of course!

Why a knight? As warriors, they need to know their tools, trust in them and train with them constantly. It helps if other, lesser knights are a bit scared of them, too.

As statesmen and emissaries, they need to know diplomacy, negotiation, and how to address both the laborer and the wealthy landowner.

And when it comes time to G.S.D. (Get S—T Done), well . . . a knight goes out there to G.S.D.

But most important is the role of the knight to the king. The king, like a business owner, is pulled and tormented by a million competing priorities. Every. Single. Day.

There is no rest. Somewhere, something is happening, and the king needs to know about it, act on it, and ultimately, win.

That's why the wisest, most powerful kings have always sought wise counsel.

I like to think business coaches, like Dan and me, are like the fabled Knights of the Round Table.

We are no-BS leaders in our own right, and our "intent" is clear. We are here to counsel the king. In our world, that's the business owner.

It's our mission to G.S.D. and to do it through sound strategy and smart, proven tactics. All while remaining in the background so the king can be the king.

Writing this, I realized that luck had never played a part in my thinking until sometime in 2009 when Dan told me that one of his nicknames was "Mr. Lucky."

Over a few beers, Dan and I talked about luck in business and in life. I wish I could tell you something earth-shattering, but it turns out, at least for the both of us, that the old Samuel Goldwyn quote is true: "the harder I work the luckier I get!"

Dan certainly works both hard and smart.

In the business of being a business coach, we read a lot. The upside of being a professional business advisor is that you have little physical inventory or capital assets. The downside is that you must carry 100% of your inventory your head!

The book you're about to read is pretty direct. A few of you may be offended. The rest of you will love it.

Dan starts where everything starts in business. It all starts with sales and leadership. You don't need an MBA to understand that if you have no sales, you have no business. Then too, if you can't lead and influence people, you can't scale or leverage your business anyway.

I've watched Dan deliver his negotiation training and his time-management modules, and I love the way he worked them into this book.

As you read, don't do it as a therapeutic escape, or you are wasting the point.

Write down action items. And then act. Knowing and not doing is the same as not doing.

What you've got in this book is "wise counsel." Please use it. Make your own luck.

If you're still reading this foreword, I think you'll not only enjoy this book, but find the momentum within it.

And, given a month or a year of applying it, you'll have your friends and colleagues asking, "What's your secret?" You just might answer, "I'm a lucky man."

Dominic Rubino
www.DominicRubino.com

Introduction

The anthem for an entrepreneur should be the timeless Bachman Turner Overdrive tune, *Takin' Care of Business*. If you don't remember it, ask Alexa or Siri to play it. She will, and you will enjoy it. You'll be dancing, I guarantee, but if you listen to the words, you'll get a suspicion that maybe the personal and professional development legends of the past, somehow implanted success suggestions into the music.

"And I'll be taking care of business (every day)
Taking care of business (every way)
I've been taking care of business (it's all mine)
Taking care of business and working overtime, workout"

Really, that about says it all. That's the reality of being in business today. You must take care of business, every day and in every way. If you're a business owner or an entrepreneur, you have the extra burden of knowing that "It's all mine!" You are the final bastion of success or failure. You have the keys to the car. What happens to your business is directly in proportion to your mindset. The work, the pressure, the finances, and all the details are all yours.

And it's not easy.

That's why this book is here. Over the years, I have consistently written blogs and articles about my ongoing experiences in the battleground of business. Sometimes, my experiences were with large businesses, sometimes small, boot-strapped business. The lessons I write about were from great successes I have had, or my clients have had, while others are about the abject failures I endured. Either way, in most cases, I was smart enough to stop and tell myself, "This is a lesson. This is a lesson. This is a lesson."

My purpose in becoming a business coach was to share those lessons with clients, groups, and audiences. All with the hope I could make a life or lives somehow better. I want to help people make more money, be happier at work, spend more quality time with their families, and just live their best possible lives instead of living in acceptance of mediocrity.

This book is divided into categories to make it easier to pick and choose a section to read that might be most applicable to your situation. Be prepared though. I do not pull punches. There is not a lot of theory here. Every page is a glimpse from lessons learned from raw-boned experience, from being on the street, winning some and losing some, but learning and growing every day.

Taking care of business!

Part
1 · · ·

Personal &
Professional Growth

The No Baloney, Bottom Line on Success!

The hardest part about achieving success is the discipline required. The foundational elements of success are straightforward and simple. It's the day-to-day commitment and discipline to make these basic elements a ritual that's tough. In fact, most people can't do it. That's why you see so few people who are exceptionally successful. The true secret to the exceptionally successful individual is

The true secret to the exceptionally successful individual is usually their soul-deep commitment to the basics and the massive action necessary. Translation: they are committed to their vision, and they work hard.

usually their soul-deep commitment to the basics and the massive action necessary. Translation: they are committed to their vision, and they work hard.

Here are what I believe are the foundational commitments and mindsets necessary for success. Keep in mind these apply without regard to location, your age, income, or education, no matter your background, and in any economy. This is where it all starts. If you are not a master of these commitments and this mindset, no fancy strategy or fads will work.

1. **Attitude**—Go ahead and laugh. Everybody says attitude

is key. The question I have is this: how many people practice having a good attitude? The Carnegie Institute says that of all the traits observed in successful people, eighty-five percent of their success is attributed to *attitude*. By the way, skills and knowledge only represent fifteen percent of the total attributes needed to achieve success.

2. **Decisiveness**—You must decide to be successful. If you're happy with where you're at right now, so be it. But if you honestly have a burning desire for the next level, commit to it or please, just shut up.

3. **Hard work**—If you want to be successful, if you want to be an entrepreneur, then know that eighty-five percent of success happens with sixty hours of work a week or more. You work forty hours a week just to get a paycheck and for survival—anything over that is what sets you up for success.

4. **Self-discipline**—Zig Zeigler once said, "If you're hard on yourself, LIFE will be easy on you." You must have the willingness to do whatever it might take to succeed (with integrity, I must add). You must be a master of self-discipline, defined long ago as, "Doing what you need to do when you need to do it, whether you want to do it or not."

5. **Set priorities**—If you start your day performing and completing a major task, the research shows you perform the rest of the day at a higher level. In turn, if you start your day with emails and trivial matters, then it is also proven that you work at a much lower level the remainder of the day. So, make the adjustment now. Start

every day with your highest-priority task. Ask yourself, "What is the consequence if I do this task or not?" If the consequences are high, do this task first. If it's a low-consequence task, simply don't do it.

6. **Single-mindedness**—It takes a minimum of five times longer to finish a job if you start, stop, start, and stop. You must put your head down and focus and get it done, eliminating any unnecessary interruptions.

7. **Open-mindedness**—You must be willing to take everything you know and potentially unlearn it, then relearn new ways of doing things. The fact is, in today's rapidly changing world, if you don't have an open mind and you continue to do business the way you've always done business, then you undoubtedly will be out of business.

8. **Risk-taking**—Sometimes you simply need to take a calculated risk. You can't be afraid. Your best opportunities may be lost simply because you took too long to think about them.

9. **Taking responsibility**—No more complaining, no more blame, no more excuses, and no more problems. A situation is only a problem if you don't learn something from it. Take charge of your life, take responsibility, and figure out a solution, learn, and move on.

10. **Be willing to change**—You must be willing and able to change, adapt, and adjust at a moment's notice. The market and consumers will not wait for you. The ability to adapt and change is imperative if you want to be an entrepreneur.

11. **Gaining total clarity**—You must constantly learn, grow, and ask questions in order to discover those elements that will affect your life and your business. Things are changing at a pace never before seen. You must examine everything, then examine it all over again. You must challenge everything, then do it again. You must question everything, again and again. Always be testing the market, reading reports, and doing market research to gain more and more clarity on your business and all that might affect it.

12. **Have written goals**—A business or person without goals—written goals—will never reach their potential. Here are the facts: seventy percent of our society don't have *any* goals. Twenty-eight percent say they have goals, but they are not written down. Two percent of the population (or less) have written goals. But here is the kicker. The two percent with written goals control more revenue than the other ninety-eight percent combined. Is that incentive enough to have clear, concise written goals?

13. **Learn to sell**—This is a requirement, a necessity with no exceptions. No matter what you think about people who sell, you had better become proficient at it. You must sell if you want to be an entrepreneur and own a business. So, read some books, take a class or seminar, hire a sales coach—do whatever you have to do, but learn to sell. It is imperative in life.

14. **Be happy**—Simply, you must love what you are doing. If you don't, it shows. So, do yourself a favor, heck, do me a favor and just get out of business. Get out of the way of others who are passionate about what they are doing and

then go find something you are, or can be, passionate about. Life is too short not to enjoy what you're doing.

Now is the time to hone your skills; it is not the time to coast. Remember, you can only coast in one direction. Never coast—you can't afford to.

Planning for Success: Purpose

I recently heard a comedian say that this year was so bad "I ordered a burger at a fast food place and the kid behind the counter asked, "Can you *afford* fries with that?"

How was this year for you and your business? That's the question every business owner is asking, or should be asking, themselves at this time of year. Unfortunately, a high percentage of business owners are afraid of the answer, many times because they don't *know* the answer, so it's easier to avoid the question.

Now is the time to face the facts. Did you have a good year? Did you have a bad year? What did you do right? What did you do wrong? What can you do better?

Now is the time to ask the questions, face the answers, and begin to plan. The time to begin planning is not annually in January; it is now.

One of my favorite quotes comes from John Richardson, American author and academic. Mr. Richardson said in 1938, "When it comes to the future, there are three kinds of people: those who let it happen, those who make it happen, and those who wonder what happened."

Which one are you?

There are an estimated two million business start-ups annually. It is estimated that nearly ninety percent will fail in two years or less. Eighty-six percent of all businesses are operating below their potential in sales and profitability. The fact is, most entrepreneurs have not really started a business but have instead created a job for themselves. A job where they are working harder, for longer hours and for less pay.

Consultants know that there are many reasons that a business might fail and most of the reasons have nothing to do with the economy, who's President, or market issues. The most common of these reasons are:

1. Lack of direction and goals

2. Impatience—they want too much too soon

3. Greed

4. Poor cost control

5. Poor quality of product

6. Insufficient capital

7. Insufficient sales

Altogether, this list simply says that businesspeople who struggle have seriously underestimated the amount of time, effort, and money required to be successful. Almost all these points come back to a significant lack of planning. So, it's time to plan, beginning now . . . beginning today. To do this, you need clarity. Without clarity, you are only working in the shadows and using best guesses—and that never works. Make a commitment to set a new path, a new discipline to raise yourself and your business to a higher plain. Otherwise, you may end next year wondering what happened . . . again.

P is for Success

Every year I try to force myself to do a ceremonial

CLEANING OF THE FILES. I go through (or at least try to) every file in every file cabinet in my two offices and recycle or throw out unnecessary paper, folders, notes, and sundry materials. It could be said that I am a hoarder of sorts with business materials. I know it sounds goofy, but I have attended or been a part of some remarkable sales, marketing, and business training in my career so far. The materials and notes from these meetings are incredibly valuable when you look at them from the perspective of their collective effect on my career. their collective effect on my career. Heck, I still have notes from sales meetings I attended in the 1970s. You never know when that information might come in handy, right?

While deep into this year's attempted purge, I came across a tattered, torn, yellowed 5"x7" file card. The writing on the card had almost faded but was still legible. Held together with tape of some kind, I could still make out the note which was important enough for me at one time to put this one concept on the card. It was titled "The 6 Ps of Personal Success."

Some people today might scoff at this kind of motivational mantra but to me and others who truly commit themselves to long-term personal growth and development, the message here is timeless. So, with that, let me share with you something from my archives.

The 6 Ps of Personal Success

1. **Purpose**—I have dedicated the time and effort to create and maintain well thought out, written goals. I have taken the same care and diligence to focus on analyzing and clearly understanding my values. These two things

will shape my future and everything I do. These goals will be the guiding light for all my future achievements.

2. **Pride**—I get up every morning with the ability to say, "I feel good about myself." I understand that I don't need the acceptance of other people to feel important. I love what I'm doing, and I am passionate about it.

3. **Patience**—I believe that things will eventually work out well. Particularly if I believe they will. I don't need everything to happen instantly.

4. **Persistence**—I stick to my purpose, especially when it seems inconvenient. I live in the immortal words of Sir Winston Churchill, "Never, Never, Never, Give Up."

5. **Perspective**—I take time to enter each day quietly, in a mood of reflection, to get focused and listen to my inner self to see things more clearly.

6. **Passion**—I am passionate about what I do every day. Passion attracts people and opportunities. Not crazy, wild-eyed passion, but passion that shows in all my actions, in everything that I do and say. The day I am not passionate about what I do, I will re-focus and find something else I can be passionate about.

I hope that this serves as a reminder that it's the simple, basic, and foundational things that will get us to where we're going faster than the latest fad.

Brush Up On Interviewing/Presentation Skills

When was the last time you interviewed for a job? For many of you, it's probably been ten or fifteen years, maybe more. Unfortunately, businesspeople sometimes have to think about looking for a job, and one thing is true: the world has changed since you last interviewed. The harsh reality is that the world does not owe you a thing for your experience and your hard work and your faithful service. There are a lot of people looking for jobs, and often they are younger and will work longer for less pay. So, if you find yourself in a situation where you must interview, you had better be sharp. The same skills apply to making a presentation when you are selling, be it a product or selling your business when you're ready to exit.

Here are essential interviewing skills you must keep in mind.

1. **Small details**—When you interview, you really should know the name of the company and its products and be able to pronounce them. Don't be the fool who starts with the question, "Can you tell me a little about your company before we get started?" Today, you should/ must know that. You have Google. You can find and learn anything you want in under a minute. Do your homework. It's the little things that will kill you in an interview, and if you don't know them . . . NEXT!

2. **Know the corporate culture**—Understand the corporate culture ahead of time, and, if nothing else, dress appropriately. But don't take any chances. Look like a pro. When you get the job, then adjust if necessary. I once had a guy show up for an interview in sunglasses and a trench coat and he never took the sunglasses off through the entire interview. Really.

3. **Kill the cell phone**—Don't check email or text during an interview or presentation. Aside from being rude, this sends the vibe that the potential employer, prospect, or

client just isn't important enough for you to actually listen to them and pay attention to what they are saying. Believe it or not, this happens. It just happened to me recently. Enough said.

4. **Breaking news**—Take time to visit the website of the company you're visiting and update yourself on the latest news and press releases that are posted. Try to be knowledgeable and don't get caught off guard. Again, do a little research.

5. **Bring work samples**—Don't be afraid to send some of your best work samples ahead of time and have extra copies with you. It matters.

6. **First impressions**—Be sure to run your cover letter and resume through spell checks and then have an eagle-eyed friend look at it as back-up. This rule applies just as much for double-checking your written or visual presentation. I've seen audience members interrupt the speaker to point out misspellings or errors in their facts during a presentation. Again, it's the little things that kill.

7. **Keep it short**—Your resume and cover letter should not be more than two pages each. Hit the highlights and leave the details for the conversation. A resume's sole purpose is to grab attention, not necessarily to sell.

8. **Play it straight**—Your cover letter and resume should be written in a clear and crisp language style with no exaggeration. Anything more and the employer will begin to second-guess your credentials. If there's any hint of fudging on work history, education or income, the deal is over.

9. **Be memorable** —Don't do so with loud coats or dresses/ outfits but with personality or listening skills or questions or work samples. There are usually plenty of people vying for every job, so figure out a logical and business savvy way to BE MEMORABLE.

10. **Say thanks, please** —As corny as it may sound, this one piece of logical etiquette is becoming a lost art. Always close with a recap of your value to the company, say you'll follow up, smile, and shake a hand and always acknowledge your appreciation of their time and interest. Then always, always, always follow up with a hand-written thank-you letter.

Always sell your value based on *what you can do now*, not necessarily what you have done for other companies.

Nobody wants to interview but if you have to, you might as well be the best person to hire. Remember these ten foundational suggestions and you'll be well on your way to a new gig.

Smart Networking or, How to Keep Networking from Being a Total Waste of Time

How's the networking going? If you say it's great, that you're getting tons of good solid leads from qualified prospects that have the complete authority to say yes, then keep doing what you're doing. You're in the minority!

Most people have no idea how they can strategically and tactically network. It's work, and it takes focus. It is not a cocktail party where you get business cards. It should be a strategic event with the goal of building your business. As such, it should be considered a powerful business activity and part of your business plan.

I believe and teach that anyone can improve their networking effectiveness by 1000%, or more, just by getting focus and clarity on exactly who their networking target is. I hope you'll spend the time to learn, clearly and concisely, exactly who your perfect target is when you are networking. If you apply this tactic, you should see a big difference in your networking results. In fact, you'll see that difference almost immediately. It's not about the *activity*, or how many events you go to, or the size of the events you go to, or even how many cards you give out and get. It's all about the *productivity* of the events you attend. Are you getting results or not?

Here Are My **9 Rules of Smart Networking**:

1. **Smart Networking #1**—The prime reason behind networking is to understand that ALL managers, executives, and business owners need to build good relationships via the people who can help them do their jobs. Connections made through effective networking can connect you with people who can do exactly that.

2. **Smart Networking #2**—Before you can ever effectively network, you must have a clear idea of who your target customer is. Take the time to succinctly define who your target prospect is for your company and sometimes for your product as well. Do this exercise often. Consumer habits are changing every day and it is imperative you know who your prospect is and how they acquire knowledge and information. Do this research twice a year. Go through client files and build a profile. Whatever you need to do, do not assume who your perfect prospect/customer is. When you do this correctly, you can now

apply tip #3.

3. **Smart Networking #3**—Only network where your top prospects network. Anything else is merely socializing. If you want to hand out your business cards to a bunch of suspects, that's up to you. However, it's much more profitable and time-efficient to hand your cards to specific prospects. This literally amounts to people who can say yes.

4. **Smart Networking #4**—Size doesn't matter. Networking at small events sometimes can be 100x more productive than big networking events. I would much rather spend my time at a smaller event where ninety percent of all attendees are my specific target, than at an event where five percent of the attendees are my target. In other words, I don't want to take the time to "find" my prospect in the crowd. I want my prospect to *be* the crowd.

5. **Smart Networking #5**—Are you just giving and getting business cards? Or, are you engaging with true prospects? Back to our central theme. If you really care about your business and your product, you will care about the time you spend wisely in the networking process. Most of you cannot afford to be networking simply for the sake of networking. If you do, then call this time spent what it is: socializing. It's happy hour with snacks, but it's not networking! For me, if I'm taking time away from my life and family, I guarantee you I'll be working. I have no time for anything else.

6. **Smart Networking #6**—It's wasted time if you're networking with anyone who can't say yes, or get you to yes! If your reason for networking is to find people who buy your product or service or those who will tell

someone to buy your product or service, then you must know that the networking event you are going to will be attended by those people. Few CEOs and senior executives go to the massive networking events. Why? Because they don't have to. They have sales teams who go to these kinds of events. So again, find out where that CEO or executive does go to network and meet peers. That's where you should be as well.

7. **Smart Networking #7**—Smart networking is all about a FOCUS on who you want to engage with and what you can accomplish when you do.

8. **Smart Networking #8**—Smart networking is all about efficiently managing your limited time by *focusing* on who and what you want. As a busy executive, manager, or business owner, it is critical to maximize the value of your time. In our existing market conditions, you cannot afford to mismanage your time by going to unproductive networking events.

9. **Smart Networking #9**—If your networking contact fits your perfect prospect/customer profile, always ask them, then and there, for an appointment to start the partnering process. If you go home to analyze, then decide they're a fit, it may already be too late to call them. Don't leave that opportunity open to the time factor.

Remember that for many industries, if not most, cold calling is dead. Mostly because the consumer will not tolerate it, plus there are extreme inefficiencies wrapped around the amount of time required to cold call. When you think about it, networking at any event when your perfect prospect is not attending too is nothing more than cold calling. Once again, the answer is simple . . . commit to SMART NETWORKING. Treat your networking time as a strategic tool. Think, plan, and be clear about your objectives. Your productivity and your profitability will grow incrementally faster than you could ever imagine. It's just good business!

The Death of Job Security

HEADLINE: JOB SECURITY IS DEAD.

Whether you're a worker, a business owner or entrepreneur, you should be afraid. The idea of creating or keeping a steady job the rest of your life is becoming a dream of the past, unless you take certain steps. The fear that surrounds this reality is impacting our economy and creating a society that is increasingly pessimistic despite living in an age of great opportunity. A Gallup Poll conducted in early 2013 stated that almost 44% of low-income American workers were afraid of losing their jobs compared to 19% in 2008.

Let's rewind three decades to a time when there was something called "job-stability" in our lives. That's when, in the post-industrial revolution era, things started changing dramatically in the global economy. Over the last two decades, we've seen America and the rest of the world live in an increasingly interdependent job market. The creation of knowledge workers, the rise of China and other developing economies, and the eroding strength of labor unions has led to an era of stiff competition and rapid scalability of new ideas. In other words, if you're not continually improving your skills and becoming more valuable to your workplace, then you're in trouble.

Irrespective of whether you are an employer or an

employee, your success today depends on how fast you learn, how you adapt, and how fast you implement ideas and new strategies in a fast-changing business landscape. The bottom line is simple: there are only two true objectives that a worker or a business owner needs to focus on: 1) To Create Value. Constantly find ways to create value for your skills, product, or service, and 2) Generate Revenue. Constantly look for ways that your skill sets, products, or services can generate revenue and how you can continually grow those skills.

That's it. Figure those questions out and you'll always have a job. Despite all this fear and pessimism, I believe there are tremendous opportunities for every individual who understands the concept of creating value and generating revenue. Remember that the definition of job security has shifted from predictable, steady streams of income to having the ability to be agile and quick to act in making your career and/or business successful. If you are an employee, job security is based on how quickly you can adapt and implement change and then thrive within that change. If you're a business owner, the same rules apply.

We are seeing new businesses form quickly and, sometimes, exit just as fast. We are seeing traditional jobs become outdated, some even disappearing altogether, while new and exciting ones are starting to crop up all the time. There are immense opportunities, guaranteed. But the difference now will always be your ability to create value and generate revenue.

It really is that simple, but for most people, it's an alien concept. However, if you focus on these two foundational issues, you'll always have a job, today and in the future. Have clarity in what you do and what you're worth to your organization. Be optimistic and work hard. But always keep an eye out for ways to increase your value in whatever you do. Never become satisfied, because if you do, you will be unemployed.

Charm Your Way to the Top and Stop Being an Introvert

If you are a person who hides in the restroom during a valuable networking event, stop it now. I guess it could be a unique strategy to meet everyone at the event, but it's not that effective.

Do you stay away from parties? Would you rather stand in a corner than participate in social settings? Even though you risk personal and professional growth, some people simply aren't built for public engagement. However, you are not alone. More than half of all of us are introverts, meaning we look inward and tend to shy away from groups of people and social gatherings.

In business, being an introvert can be an advantage as well as a disadvantage. Many people associate success in business with being expressive, sometimes bombastic, and lively in conversations and in dealings. These are the extroverts, the opposite of introverts.

However, in recent years, we've seen a radical shift in our attitude towards introversion. With a slight switch in their frame of mind, introverts can add charisma, join a lively conversation, and then you can always crawl back into your shell.

In business, we often see leaders who are introverts. They might be sharp, data-driven managers but take them to a meeting and ask them to give a presentation in front of a group and they might blow the whole thing.

Lisa Petrilli, Sr., marketing and strategy executive and author of the book *An Introvert's Guide to Networking* has interesting views on being an introvert and successfully networking. Growing up, she was shy and had a deep aversion to networking. She avoided any outside events. However, she soon knew that to succeed, she had to change, so she started using simple but effective tactics. The first tactic was to realize that there was nothing wrong with being an introvert. Introversion is simply a characteristic that allows people to return to their own quiet moments of working with ideas. According to Petrilli, successful introverts are some of the best relationship builders in one-on-one settings.

Another great book about networking as an introvert is Dorothy Tannahill-Moran's book *Easier Networking for Introverts and the Socially Reluctant*. Tannahill-Moran has an entire series directed at how to be successful in business as in introvert.

If you think you are an introvert, here are some tips to get you started in being a charismatic leader. First, accept your characteristic trait of introversion but be willing to adapt as necessary. Step out of your shell when needed and meet and greet people with a big smile and a firm handshake. Attend networking events important for building your career. Purposefully change your attitude about how you view relationship building. Remember, every move you make will have a positive impact on your career. You do not need to be an "artificial extrovert," to succeed in today's business world. You can also reach out to people using LinkedIn, Twitter, Facebook, and other social media tools to help you overcome your fears.

Introverts who do not network are making a huge dent in their career growth. Pace yourself between networking events, re-energize by going back to your mode of introversion but spring back into the charismatic leader you want to be.

Face the Facts

Do you ever talk to yourself? I have chats with myself all the time. Sometimes, even in public. I talk to myself about all sorts of things. But there are only a few questions I have worked hard to make it a habit to ask myself consistently and persistently. "Habit" is the key word here. You must have the discipline to regularly ask yourself questions that make you uncomfortable because you're afraid of the answers. Most of us take the easy way out and repeatedly lie to ourselves. When we are forced to unveil or admit to a "personal growth" opportunity, it's just too easy to blow it off, walk away and ignore the potential implications. Admit it. It's much easier to look in a mirror and lie to yourself and avoid the challenge than it is to accept what the truth might be. What we need is to realistically use old-fashioned personal and honest evaluation and self-talk.

Now calm down. I'm not talking about therapeutic, clinical evaluation and years of therapy. What I am talking about is just taking the time, every once in a while, to take a deep breath and, as Zig Ziglar used to say, "Give yourself a checkup from the neck up." It's a simple personal assessment, the kind of assessment I believe will extend your career and possibly your life.

One of the primary questions that should be at the top of this list should always be, "Am I still enthusiastic about what I'm doing today?" It's the question that challenges our enthusiasm for our career and life. Harvey Mackay, the noted author, columnist, speaker, and businessman says, "One of life's great tragedies is the curiosity, enthusiasm, and excitement about life that we are born with, seems to erode as the years go by." He goes on to say, "When the challenges of life get in the way, it's easy to spend more energy on putting out little fires than on sparking enthusiasm for overcoming the challenge."

We're not talking about fanatical, wide-eyed, standing-on-chairs, screaming-from-the-mountain-top kind of enthusiasm. What I'm talking about is that natural, confident look and feel, that aura that radiates from anyone who loves, really loves, and believes in what they are doing, or are about to do, and why they are doing it.

More than anything else, I believe people buy from and work with people who are enthusiastic about what they represent. The day is over when people will ONLY buy for "the solution." Today there are too many choices and options, too much uncertainty, too much change. So, the difference in making the sale of a product, service, idea, or yourself, is quickly turning into an issue of whether our prospects and customers believe in your enthusiasm. I guarantee you they are asking their own ultimate decision-making question: "Who among my choices do I really feel and believe is the most enthusiastic about their own products or service?" That's who they want to work with.

Many years ago, Henry Ford, a guy who did pretty well for himself, probably summed up the importance of ENTHUSIASM best when he said, "You can do anything if you have enthusiasm. Enthusiasm is the spark in your eye, the swing in your gait, the grip of your hand, the irresistible surge of your will and your energy to execute your ideas. Enthusiasm is at the bottom of all progress. With it, there is accomplishment. Without it, there are only alibis."

So, what's your story? The question of enthusiasm might be more important today than ever before. However, the question is time-tested and applied for generations. It is one of the keys to success of any kind. Believe me, if you don't believe in yourself everyone can tell . . . and someone is always watching. Let's step up and face the facts. Love what you're doing or stop. You'll do everyone around you a favor.

Finding Your Personal Yoda

Ahh, a moment of peaceful contemplation. A poetic ambition, I must say, but not always realistic in most people's lives. I did have a few minutes this week where I took the time to take a deep breath and discuss with myself how I've managed to succeed to the levels I have. I thought about those daring individuals who helped me overcome adversity, achieve success, and gain clarity in my career and business ventures. Sometimes they had the guts to kick my butt around the block to get my attention. Looking back, most were more of a personal success "sponsor", my personal Yoda, instead of a mentor.

Just like Luke Skywalker had his Yoda, we should hope to be lucky enough to have a personal sponsor. So, who is a sponsor? According to a blog by Sylvia Ann Hewlett titled *The Real Benefit of Finding a Sponsor*, in the January 2011 issue of the *Harvard Business Review* in, a sponsor is someone who "uses chips on his or her protégé's behalf and advocates for his or her next promotion as well as doing at least two of the following: expanding the perception of what the protégé can do; making connections to senior leaders; promoting his or her visibility; opening up career opportunities; offering advice on appearance and executive presence; making connections outside the company; and giving advice." Yep, people like this were my sponsors.

Hewlett differentiates between mentors—people who most often simply provide friendly advice—and sponsors, who are those who root for you and help you reach the next level. My sponsors often had skin in the game and made me more accountable than those mentors who provided great advice and direction. I've had the good fortune of interacting with both, but acquiring a sponsor often gets us the "Godfathers" who can help us succeed.

In today's quick and cutthroat business world, it is imperative that you find a great mentor. Find someone who can take you under his or her wings and truly enable you to be accountable in your life and business. As a protégé, you have the responsibility to work hard and follow through on your sponsor's guidelines. They've vouched for you, thus creating a powerful level of accountability.

Sponsors often volunteer to teach you what they know and narrate their own life experiences to you. They're interested in passing their legacy on to the next generation. You can call on a sponsor daily and receive coaching and advice without questions. A sponsor believes in you. They have put their reputation on the line for your career success and growth. A great sponsor can provide you with a perfect guidance system for your future.

In my life, I've had the great fortune of having several mentors/sponsors. I'm just now beginning to realize what that meant to my life and career. An admiral in the Navy; a

Fortune Five CEO; a world-renowned speaker and trainer; a relative; and a farmer all sponsored and mentored me and introduced me to key people within their network. They trusted me, opened their networks for me, taught and advised and counseled me, and believed in my future success.

So, how do you find a sponsor? The first step is to look within your life. Who are the most successful people you know, or would like to know, who command the greatest respect from peers and subordinates? Who are the ones who show great leadership skills, value people, and understand business and the world well?

Open your eyes for individuals already within your current contacts and ask to talk. Tell them about your immediate and future goals and ask them if they would be willing to mentor you and guide your career. Often, sponsors will get you on a great career track and quickly provide you with solid advice and guidance.

You can also seek sponsors within your industry. Look for top-performing individuals who display excellent character, outstanding leadership skills, and possess stellar reputations. Just one person who will agree to help can open vast networks and change your life.

However, always remember that this is a commitment and a huge responsibility on your part. It is totally up to you to honor this relationship with hard work and perseverance. If you are not prepared to focus, listen, and follow through on your sponsor's advice, the road ahead could get bumpy, and your sponsor/mentor won't be around for long. The commitment is one that will be sacred. Remember, your sponsor is committing their name to the brand that is YOU!

If you need help finding your sponsor, give me a call or

send me a note.

Life Lessons, So Far

Sometimes it takes a lifetime of lessons to learn the things that would have made the life lived, so far, better. Recently I was asked, "What five suggestions would you make to begin improving oneself?" I thought, *This will be easy.* But it wasn't. Not when I took into consideration all the twists and turns life had dished up so far, all the mistakes I'd made, all the successes I'd had, and what, in retrospect, I'd learned.

The one thing I know for a fact is that self-improvement should never end. From cradle to grave, we need to understand that we must continually be on a path of self-improvement. You can't really get away from it. If you choose to be homeless and live on the streets or be a hermit and live in the woods, you still must learn how to do that. Even that requires some level of self-improvement. If you believe you need to "begin" improving yourself, I will ask you to review your life so far, as I think you will discover you've already been doing something towards that objective. Simply thinking about improving oneself IS a beginning.

My list turned out to be about as foundational as you can get. If you're just embarking on a lifelong, dedicated journey of self-improvement, be sure you master the basics first. Here's my starter list:

1. **Prioritize everything you do.** Make it a habit to only do the most important things in life. You will eventually realize you didn't need to try to do everything. You just needed to learn to do the most important things. Those things with the highest consequence. Forget about everything else. People will tell me they would do things

they know would improve their lives if they just had the time. Well, listen close . . . you do have the time. I've found that about eighty percent of a person's time each day is wasted on unimportant, low-priority tasks. Are you investing your time? Or, are you wasting your time?

2. **Read.** Honestly, I don't care what you're reading, but set time aside every day to read. The average American reads two books a year. That's it. We have our faces shoved so far into our cell phones; laptops and video games that we've forgotten how to learn and how to communicate. Mix a self-improvement book or educational CD with a novel—however you want to do it—and read. We spend the equivalent of two semesters of college just in windshield time in our cars every year. Take that time to go to Automobile University. Listen to a CD and learn a new language, learn a life skill, or listen to a book.

3. **Learn to listen.** The lost art in business is the art of listening. No one listens anymore. An expert recently commented that most people only listen to find their chance to talk next. If you take the time to listen, you will thrive, and you will learn. Listen to those around you. Listen to the people you work with. Listen to your friends and family. If you really want to begin improving yourself immediately, start listening. You'll be amazed at what you will hear.

4. **Learn to sell.** No matter what you're doing in life or hope to do, you will need to have the skill to sell something to others. Like it or not, everyone sells, and everyone will have to sell. Learn this as soon as you can. Take a Sales 101 course, read a sales book, listen to a CD on sales

or take an online course, but do whatever you have to do to learn the basics of sales. Whether you're selling as a profession or just want to sell yourself better when asking for a raise, learn how to sell, NOW.

5. **Learn to learn from mistakes.** Some people allow mistakes to stagnate and ruin their lives. They give up and quit trying. Many companies spend millions of dollars just to uncover who made mistakes. The first is stupid, and the other is a waste of time. Learn from mistakes and move on. Mistakes are a way of life. Thomas Watson of IBM fame was once asked his take on how a person could improve their rate of success. His answer was "improve your rate of failure." A mistake is only a true mistake if you did not learn from it. I have a four-step process I teach all my coaching clients when they're dealing with mistakes:

- What happened? (Honestly analyze what really happened.)

- How did it happen? (What went wrong?)

- How can you prevent this from ever happening again? (What is the solution?)

- Move on. Know what you've learned and apply it.

The road to self-improvement can begin by simply deciding to take that lifelong journey. The key to its success— as with anything—is your commitment, dedication, and the discipline to do the work. So, you must ask yourself, *how important is this?* Your answer will direct the rest of your life.

Grandpa's Rules:
A Farmer's Rules for Success in Life and Business

I always smile when I think of him—and I think of him often. Perry Gilbert (P.G.) Harris was my grandfather.

In my life I've had the pleasure of meeting, working with, or mentoring under legendary personal and business development minds. I've learned a ton from their teaching. But my value system and my work ethic come directly from the teaching of my grandfather, P.G. Harris. He was a farmer—a wheat farmer, to be exact—in Sumner County, in the state of Kansas, USA.

The landscape was the stuff of poems and songs, rolling prairie as far as the eye can see, and wheat fields that stretched for miles and miles. And P.G. Harris fit the landscape. He was tall, lanky, and tough. He always wore bib overalls, always had a farmers' tan, and wore farmer's boots and a farmer's hat. My grandfather worked about 600 acres of wheat and pastureland and I worked with him from the time I was old enough to work. He was a successful farmer and a good businessman. And he had rules. As I grow older and began to reflect on life, I also began to realize Grandpa's rules applied to more than farming. They applied to the art of business and life. As an adult, I realized I had taken his rules and adapted them to modern-day business applications. So far, I have noted sixteen of "Grandpa's Rules" that I've adapted and use every day.

For the sake of brevity, here are seven of the Grandpa Rules:

1. **(EFFORT) "Hard work never hurt anyone so get busy."**

   He taught me my most valuable skill to this day, and that

was the importance of having a powerful work ethic. I believe a work ethic is one of the most desired skills an employer looks for. Too many people just don't get it and want big pay for little effort, and that's not the formula for success in this life. In fact, I believe a solid work ethic is an important *skill* that employers find extremely valuable.

2. **(GOALS) "The world doesn't owe you a thing; you've got to earn it."**

Congratulations if your family has money or if you've won the lottery, but if you wait for the phone to ring with your "big" opportunity, you'll be standing in the welfare line. It's important to learn early that you will *earn* everything that you get in life through gaining clarity about what you want out of life, then you must add in hard work, dedication, focus, commitment, passion, discipline, and an ongoing personal development program. The adage is still as true today as it was a hundred years ago: *The harder you work the luckier you get.*

3. **(PRIDE) "Whatever you do in life, whatever it is, be the best. If you're a ditch digger for the county, you had better win the award for the best ditch digger in the county."**

There is a certain amount of pride that defines a job well done. This mirrors your level of personal values and honor and will reflect on you for years to come. Basically, if you're in a job you don't like for whatever reasons, you have two choices. The first is to slack off, work halfheartedly and gripe and moan about the boss, the job, the business, co-workers, and on and on. Or, according to Grandpa's teachings, just shut up and do your job and do it well. Even though you might not enjoy what you're doing, you owe the company a day of focused work, even your best work, without complaint. They're still paying you, right? Then, when you can, you find something different to do. Be proud of what you're doing even if it's not ideal. The right people will always eventually notice which choice you make.

4. **(QUALITY) "The job isn't complete until it's done right."**

In a certain part of Kansas, this statement is known as "Perry's Rule." To this day it is still referred to. It doesn't matter if you've been working all day and you're tired. You should never be satisfied with a job that's incomplete or just pieced together. The only job that is truly done and complete, and one you can be proud of, is one that's done right. So, according to the rule, you do the work until it is done right.

5. **(EFFORT) "Never do a job "half-fast."**

Granddad would tolerate my mistakes, bad judgment, and plain old screw-ups as long as I was working hard and working at full speed. This rule revolved around the idea that all is forgivable if you worked hard, and you learned something from the issue. However, he had no time for problems caused by mistakes when someone was moving slow, half-hearted, without purpose or initiative, or "half-fast" (read between the lines).

6. **(ACCOUNTABILITY) "Your word is your bond."**

Your value as a human being is based on the value of your word. If you said you were going to do something, then he expected you to do it. If you agreed on a time to meet or a time to start, he expected you to be there. If you broke that promise, he expected you to fix it. If you shook hands on a deal, he expected you to stand by it. If you didn't, you seldom got more chances. The world would be a better place if everyone held themselves accountable.

7. (EMPATHY) "Look for the good in everyone."

Grandpa's message was simple. It's easy to find fault in people. This approach always leads to ridicule and negative relations. I never once heard him say a bad word about anyone, ever. He lived his belief. He always looked through the potential negatives and looked for a good and common ground.

In 1971, I was one of the first young people to come home from college with long hair. This discretion caused quite the uproar in my small town, to the point where my father told me to get a haircut or leave. I was upset and jumped in my car and, as requested, left. On the way out of town, I stopped by the farm to get counsel from Grandpa. I asked him what he thought about the issue. I will never forget what he told me. True to his rules he looked at me and said, "I guess it's what's under the hair that counts."

Today, over forty years later, ironically, I have no hair, but I think about that line nearly every day of my life. It's about tolerance and seeing the good in people beyond the physical. The foundational truths to Grandpa's Rules apply to success in business today as much as success in life. And, as I do what I do, I will continue to live and teach, with pride, "Grandpa's Rules."

It's Not Easy Being Lucky

I've concluded that there is no such thing as luck. It's an interesting concept, one that has been discussed for ages. In the first century AD, Roman philosopher, Seneca, said, "Luck is what happens when preparation meets opportunity." Our third U.S. President, Thomas Jefferson, said, "I'm a great believer in luck, and I find the harder I work, the more I have of it."

Good luck is something you can create for yourself. Some would say I've been a lucky guy. However, every person I've ever met who is consistently successful was told at some point in time they were "just lucky" . . . no skill involved, just lucky. Sometimes that can get downright irritating. No matter the sacrifices you've made, the "above and beyond" things you've done to prepare for an opportunity, some jealous soul, somewhere, will say "you're lucky!"

So, I've examined what it takes to achieve the ranking of being "lucky" and I've come to learn that you must *earn the right* to be lucky. I've created a list of things you must do to become one of the luckiest people you know.

- You must work harder than anyone else in your industry

- You must be disciplined, doing things you need to do, when you must do them, whether you want to or not

- You must be committed to task prioritization, time management, and planning for your coming day

- If you're in sales, you need to talk to at least fifty percent more prospects than your peers

- If you're in sales, you need to directly ask your prospects to buy early and often

- You must always "over-deliver" the expectations of your customers

- You must have an ongoing personal education program no matter how old you are

- You must have clear and concise personal and business goals

- You must read those goals every day

- You must track your progress or lack thereof

- Did I mention that you must work really, really, really, really hard?

I'm always trying to get better at life and at what I do. Today, mediocre isn't good enough. Many will argue that luck will play a big part in your success. But luck results from the position you've created for yourself.

It's not easy to be lucky. You must be disciplined with the grit to simply persevere, and the bottom line seems to be *it's always better to work hard with determination and focus, long enough to be lucky.*

No Market for Bad Attitudes

People with negative attitudes wear me out. After they wear me out, they piss me off. I just don't get it. If you're in business and you want to stay in business, there is no room for a negative outlook in today's market. A business owner cannot afford to behave like this. I have seen a bad attitude stand out as the single reason someone lost their business. It permeates and sets a tone for a business, good or bad. Your customers *will* feel the vibe. Your attitude directly affects your staff, the atmosphere of your office/or business, and

> *... it's always better to work hard with determination and focus, long enough to be lucky.*

your customers. Your customers and prospects won't stand for a negative attitude. Why? They don't have to. There are far too many alternative choices for them, so they'll just go somewhere else. They don't have to put up with a bad attitude they can avoid just by going somewhere else or by accessing the internet.

In my business coaching practice, I see it every day and it can be fatal for a business owner and their business. So, it's time for some "mental triage." As a business coach, I look for a few key symptoms of what the great Zig Ziglar called "Stinkin' Thinkin'."

The businessperson is:

1. Always tired and worn out

2. There are ALWAYS problems

3. They blame everyone else for everything that's wrong instead of taking personal responsibility

4. They blame the economy for all their collective woes

5. They are overtly emotional

6. They are working from a business strategy of survival only. (I know this from experience. I worked with a customer whose initial goal for his business

was to, "Get up in the morning, go to work, and do everything possiblve to break even."

If you find yourself checking off these items, here are a few solutions:

1. Force yourself to take some quiet time every day to just meditate and relax.

2. Get your time under control and prioritize your tasks. Only do those things with the highest consequences and do them first.

3. Start taking responsibility for mistakes, shortcomings, failures and, yes, your successes, too.

4. Set written goals. Understand what is important and what you're working for—every succcssful businessperson today has clear written goals.

5. Plan a strategy of thriving, versus just surviving. It's a completely different mindset.

6. Get new friends and associates. If everyone you hang with is always bitching and moaning, you will too. Surround yourself with positive input.

7. Get some coaching. There is a reason all top-level professional athletes have a coach. It just makes sense that businesses should, too.

8. Plan your business and your life basing all strategies on *what versus what is if*. Don't worry about the "what ifs" of life; don't ruin your life because you're in a panic about what *might* happen. Understand the situation and how it is affecting you right now, then plan your strategies on that reality.

As Henry Ford said a long time ago, "If you think you can, or you can't—you're right." Think positive thoughts . . . life is more fun that way.

So, You Want to be Wealthy?

Just as the old blues song goes, "Everyone wants to go to heaven, but nobody wants to die." So too goes wealth. It seems everyone wants to be rich, but few want to work for it. The best way to control your destiny and to build personal equity is to work for yourself.

In today's economy, jobs are precious and the "protected" job is something of a dinosaur. You can bust your buns with long work weeks, non-stop travel, and cutbacks that just mean more stress and work for the survivors. You must get yourself into a situation where you control your destiny. It's getting scary when companies cut staff hours to twenty-nine hours a week so they don't have to pay benefits. Or when loyal employees are laid off weeks before retirement benefits kick in. In some highly publicized cases, long-term employees lost everything because of fat-cat mismanagement.

One solution is if you're willing to work hard for someone else, you should be willing to work hard for yourself. Find something that turns you on, that you are interested in, and then think. That's right, think about how you might make a living by doing that job.

The job that was perfect for me was business coaching. It feels like the last thirty-five years of my career was a "dress rehearsal" for becoming a successful business coach. I own my own business, and, through hard work and sacrifice, I have built a strong and successful practice. I control my destiny.

Brian Tracy recently published a short article on the ways to become wealthy. I think it ties in nicely to what we're discussing here. So, here it is. Enjoy and take heed to the message.

Success: Believe It or Not

Someone, please, help me understand.

Over the last forty years or so, I've been in the business world, working, observing, studying, teaching, training, and coaching. This entire time I've continually reviewed and studied countless books and articles, research, reports, and more research in search of the secrets of success. Repeatedly, there have been some basic elements that always emerge. Every time, without fail, these basic elements of success reveal themselves. So why do we not learn? Why do we not take notice and pay attention to these recurring success secrets? I think it's because we are gluttons for punishment. We seem to thrive in insanity, doing the same things over and over again, expecting different results.

The most basic of these recurring elements revolves around people's personal belief structure. Henry Ford said, as I've mentioned before and paraphrase here, "If you think you can, or think you can't, you're right." Brian Tracy, in his *Financial Success* newsletter calls this the *Law of Belief.* It comes down to this: Whatever you believe, with feeling, becomes your reality. In other words, whatever you intensely and passionately believe becomes your reality. Successful people block out and consistently work on not allowing any negative forces to enter their world. Mr. Tracy goes on to say, ". . . they will not entertain, think about, or talk about any possibility that they'll fail. They do not even think about the possibility of failure."

Sometimes this is called Positive Knowing vs. Positive Thinking. Positive thinking is trying hard to think positive with quite a lot of wishing, dreaming, and mental trickery

> *Positive Knowing is when a person can absolutely and passionately know that whatever happens personally in business, in the economy, in the world . . . no matter what, they WILL be successful. This is accomplished only with an unwavering willpower.*

going on. However, Positive Knowing is when a person can absolutely and passionately know that whatever happens personally in business, in the economy, in the world . . . no matter what, they WILL be successful. This is accomplished only with an unwavering willpower. Willpower drives your confidence; it is the fuel for your success engine. Brian Tracy says, "Willpower is essential for success. Willpower is based on confidence. It's based on conviction. It's based on faith. It's based on your belief in your ability to triumph over all obstacles."

With so much negativity going on throughout our world, your success can be a simple as adjusting the level of belief you have in yourself. If you're surrounded by negative co-workers, get away from them. If you're surrounded by negative friends, find new friends. If you're in a negative job setting, change it or go somewhere else. You must believe in yourself, and you must create a support network that believes in you and what you're trying to accomplish. I firmly believe we are now living in the ultimate "Is the glass half full or half empty" point in time. *Survivor mentalities* say the glass is half empty. *Thriving mentalities* no longer say it's half full, but say the glass is neither half full nor half empty, because the glass can be refilled!

I met a businessperson last week who moaned about how bad the economy was and I asked, "Realistically, how much has the economy hurt your business?" He looked me straight in the eye and said, "Well it really hasn't yet, but it will." In every recessionary economy there are opportunities for those who believe enough to see the opportunities. The author, T. Harv Eker of *The Millionaire Mind* fame suggests it's the viewpoint of understanding the difference between *what vs. what is if.* Be realistic and honest about *what is.* Use, *what is, as your foundation for reality. To simply smile and steadfastly hold to your beliefs and willpower, even when others are negative.* Do that with confidence and your success will blossom while others will continue to wonder what your secret is.

Success Requires Three Bones

I'm always intrigued how people will express what it takes to be successful. I came across a great definition a few weeks ago that I love. It really captures the essence of what is required to be successful at anything. This quote comes from Kobi Yamada, President and CEO of Compendium,

Inc. who says, "Success requires three bones, the *wishbone*, the *backbone* and the *funny bone.*"

Funny and true, so let's break it down.

The Wishbone—The wishbone gives us the ability to visualize the future, to be able to dream without restrictions or constraints. It gives us the ability to see what our possibilities and potential are, the opportunity to be able to develop a life plan through possibility-thinking and goal setting, and the ability to unabashedly dream of what could be. In goal-setting exercises, I challenge my business coaching customers with the question, "How big would you *allow* yourself to dream if you knew you could not fail?" You might be surprised at the number of people who restrict themselves and undermine their potential by not allowing themselves to dream.

The great American philosopher and humorist, Mark Twain once said, "Twenty years from now, you will be more disappointed by the things you didn't do than by the ones you did. So, throw off the bowlines, sail away from the safe harbor, catch the trade winds in your sails. Explore. Dream. Discover."

The Backbone—The backbone represents the importance of taking risks and having the nerve to take chances. The backbone means having the ability and drive to stick to the job, to have massive confidence in what you're doing . . . then to step out in faith when the world keeps throwing up roadblocks.

Winston Churchill said, "Success is going from failure to failure without loss of enthusiasm." He added, "It is never possible to guarantee success, it is only possible to deserve it."

The Funny Bone—And finally, and probably most

important of all—the funny bone. In business or in life, it is imperative that you can laugh at yourself. I had to break out of my "superego" mold and learn to laugh at my mistakes instead of dwelling on them. Heck, I've made so many mistakes in life that I can say I'm a funny guy. Not being able to laugh at life and learn from it equals an unhappy, pressure-filled, and unfulfilling life. Believe me, life is much too short to deprive yourself of the humor life has to offer. And as an entrepreneur, businessperson, or parent, learning to laugh is mandatory.

It all goes back to attitude and how you take both the highs and the lows of business and life. It's the *attitude of gratitude*. It's the glass-half-full concept. It's what Zig Ziegler calls *"stinkin' thinkin'"* versus "possibility thinking."

Yes, our world is a serious place, and yes, we must focus and work hard and all that, but from personal experience, it's also good to learn to lighten up, stop and take a deep breath, laugh a little and not let the steam build. The great golfer, Payne Stewart once said, "If you can't laugh at yourself, then how can you laugh at anybody else? I think people see the human side of you when you do that." And, my friends, as far as I'm concerned, that's what the world needs a lot more of these days. Show your family, friends, colleagues, and customers that you are humble enough to laugh a little bit at yourself. It makes life and business much easier.

The Best Habit

I just love to answer questions that make me think, really think, about the answer. Someone recently asked me what the best habit was that I have ever learned from another person and then took for my own. It took some time to consider this, but the answer was simple. This was a "habit" I learned as a young man growing up on a wheat farm in south-central Kansas. My grandfather, P. G. Harris was a farmer and a quiet, lead by example, kind of man. He didn't say much, but when he did, you had better be listening. That habit of leading by example, an attitude he lived by and taught, I now see as a skill that represented his philosophy on success at any level. He was my greatest inspiration in life. My grandfather taught me the value and power of a work ethic. The power of mastering a work discipline is something that has been a powerful skill for me my entire life and career. I've been involved in starting fourteen businesses; turned around over 400; have hired hundreds of people over the years; and I'm a Business Coach who helps business owners, executives, and entrepreneurs worldwide. Believe me, a work ethic is a powerful skill, and sometimes seems it seems rare.

Many of my successes have come from simply being willing to outwork the competition. So many people today have an attitude of complacency, believing the world owes them something. They sit back and wait for success to come to them. The focus of one of the greatest business and personal development books of all time, *Think and Grow Rich*, by Napoleon Hill was in short, *"What you think about most of the time you become."* Basically, you have total control over the activation of your own Law of Attraction, based on how you think. You will attract positive and negative things, people and opportunities in your life based totally upon how you think. So, if you think possibilities or you think survival, that's the opportunities and the people you will attract. One requires little to partial effort (survival thinking), the other, *possibility thinking*, requires massive action. In other words, it requires work. Focused, hard work. Having a vision; setting goals; managing daily priorities; accomplishing high-consequence tasks; and all the other things involved with success require work.

Understand this: if you're not willing to do what is necessary to get the job done, it's your responsibility to clearly understand this and accept this. Once you do, SHUT UP. If you're not willing to put the work in, quit complaining. I don't want to hear it.

I'm sick of it.

It's not the fault of the government, high taxes, the world situation, the weather, or your dog. Understand this—it's your choice to not to put in the effort, and if that is the case, clearly understand your decision and choice, and get out of the way of the people who are willing to put in the effort.

My grandfather's rule was this: "The job isn't done until it's done right, and you don't stop until it's done right." This attitude, derived from learning discipline, is the only difference between good and great. A strong work ethic often outweighs gender, background, education, and all other factors. It's always been the one thing that set me apart . . . and I'm thankful for learning the lesson such a long time ago from my grandfather.

Go here to get your free checklist for choosing a business coach:

businesscoachdan.com/straighttalk

Part 2

Entrepreneurship

Are You Nuts?

Have you ever shared a dream or goal with someone you love or trust, and they looked back with a smile to say, "You're nuts! That's crazy. You can't do that."

Over the years, I've observed the one thing that hinders the potential success, is how a person might answer one question. In fact, I always ask my business coaching clients this question as we lay down goals and objectives and structure a vision for their business. The question is, "What could you accomplish if no one told you it was impossible?" Sounds simple, doesn't it? So many people have literally forgotten how to dream. They've restricted their potential, based on their perceived restrictions and constraints.

Think about that for a moment. How many of your dreams and ambitions have been abandoned because someone else told you what you wanted to do couldn't be accomplished? Maybe they said things like, "You're nuts if you try to start a business today. The economy is too bad!" or "That's a terrible idea for a product/business. Are you nuts?"

Okay, you guessed it, I'm on the "positive attitude" bandwagon again, but it is a proven strategy. Without it, nothing is possible. The late actor, inspirational speaker, and activist, Christopher Reeve said, "So many of our dreams at first seem impossible, then they seem improbable, and then, when we summon the will, they soon become inevitable."

In his recent newspaper column, businessman and author Harvey Mackay reminds us that "What we call progress was once called impossible. If necessity is the mother of invention, then a positive attitude is the master of the impossible!" A positive attitude is so important for believing in the "possible." Disney (famously) makes it a point of strategic pride to tell employee "Imagineers" that they need to explore possibilities and never accept boundaries or limitations on their imagination.

To be successful in business today, in fact, to survive in business, we must begin and end every day exploring the boundaries of what is possible. We must continually challenge ourselves and have a positive outlook about innovation, creativity, growth, personal development, and potential. We must develop and nurture a vision of the future and a positive expectation when problem-solving. Plus, we must continually challenge ourselves to understand what the realities of all situations are versus what the general perceptions are!

This is not a new idea—the concept has been around a long, long time. A classic business book, *Think and Grow Rich* by Napoleon Hill, dedicates much of the text to this specific subject. And this incredible book was written all the way back in 1937. Don't let any "dream vampires" suck the life out of your hopes, ambitions, and desires. Stand tall and hold on to your aspirations for all you're worth and let no one stand in the way of something you believe in, or for that matter, someone you believe in.

It's hard, but you can do it.

Just promise me one thing . . . the next time someone asks you the question, "Are you nuts?" Make it a point to smile, then laugh and look them straight in the eye and say, "Probably."

So, You Say You're an Entrepreneur?

I spoke recently about why I don't have hair. And, just

to be clear, I still don't have hair. This is a fact, and it is true mostly because there are several things that tick me off enough to continue to pull my hair out. There are a few things, specifically, that just drive me batty, make my eyes roll and my stomachache.

The fact is, that I would rather kiss my great Aunt Betty on the lips than listen to another person tell me they are an ENTREPRENEUR, when in fact, they absolutely do not have a glimmer of an idea, not even a slight hint, what that term means. For that matter, some of those people don't even know how to spell it.

Some people think the word entrepreneur is a cool way to describe themselves. Look, just because you have a great idea and a pickup truck doesn't mean you're an entrepreneur. For those of you who really are entrepreneurs, you understand that the term should not be thrown around so lightly. The title of entrepreneur is one that is earned and worn proudly. It is earned with sweat and tears, heartache, and devastating failures that are hopefully counterbalanced with remarkable and incredible successes. But you're picking a fight if you take the term lightly around someone who has paid the price.

Bloomberg reports that eight of ten "entrepreneurs" (some will say even more) who start a business will fail within the first eighteen months. Are you kidding me? This eighty-percent failure rate is a staggering statistic that should be revealed on fifty-foot banners outside every business school in the country. How can this happen? I believe the answer is simple. The fact is that most entrepreneurs, and "wanna be" entrepreneurs who start a business today simply are not mentally prepared. They dive into business totally blind and do not understand how the world, let alone the world of business, works. They don't understand that starting a business has much more to do with will and effort, mindset and attitude, endurance, and sheer willpower, and understanding acceptable risk, than it does with spreadsheets.

In an article on *Entrepreneur.com* by Steve Tobak, he made a powerful statement on this exact subject. He said, "Life offers two distinct paths for each of us. The first is the path of least resistance: Get a job, show up, and collect your paycheck, rinse, and repeat. The second path is the risky one: Take chances, face enormous challenges, suffer terrible defeat, rise up even stronger than before, and someday make it big. If you choose the latter path, I can say one thing for sure: there will be desperate times. But contrary to what you might think, those are the most precious times. When you're desperate, when you feel you have nothing to lose, when you're most open to opportunity and change, that's when great ventures are born."

That is the life of a true entrepreneur. This is a life of knowing that not everything you do will pan out like you thought it would. This is a life about learning to survive the failures that will happen so you can experience the big wins and truly enjoy and revel in the successes.

For those who have earned their entrepreneurial battle scars, you can help. Don't be shy about giving advice and some survival tips to the new kids on the block. If they're willing to take it, give them a hand and sometimes a kick in the pants. Mentorship has played an incredibly important role in my life. If it has in your life, too, give some of that back.

If you think you have what it takes intellectually, mentally, and physically, then welcome to the ranks of the intrepid entrepreneur. Make a run at it and give me a call in eighteen months to let me know how you're doing.

Are You Committed to Success?

The situation comes straight out of children's storybooks. Remember the story about Henny Penny, the little chicken who made great bread? Everyone wanted to eat it, but no one wanted to help make it.

The story plays out every day in the real world when it comes to how business owners, entrepreneurs, and executives alike feel about success and what it takes to get it. Everybody wants it, but not everybody is willing to work for it.

If you conducted a survey asking people if they wanted to be successful, I would take Las Vegas odds on the fact that all of them would say yes. However, if you change the question and ask, "Are you willing to commit to success and make any and every sacrifice necessary to be successful?" my guess is the answer would change by about 98%, meaning that most would question the meaning of sacrifice, would want to think about it, or would just say no.

People all want the spoils but are not willing to do what it takes to achieve at high levels. This is especially tough for people who think they are entrepreneurs, and many who have bought a franchise. Often, these people come from successful corporate environments where they have budgets, reputations—did I say BUDGETS—marketing teams, sales teams, and more. Then they go out on their own with only their thick resume from corporate successes. When they must put in the time and effort to do the work on their own, they either don't know what to do or aren't willing to do what is necessary once that becomes apparent.

I have had people during business coaching sessions, and in some of my seminars and workshops, ask me what it takes, what is the secret to success, particularly entrepreneurial success. I tell them the first secret is the simplest secret: You must work very, very, very, very, very, very hard . . . and smart!

The second secret is, repeat the first secret!

Some will give me a knowing smile. Others will give me the "stink eye" and then complain that I'm holding back and not sharing the "real" secrets. I even had a guy once who looked at me and in a dejected manner and said, "I'm not willing to work that hard."

Either way, they know I'm right.

I don't care what kind of degrees you have or from where. I don't care who your family is or what your name is. I don't care whether you were born rich or poor. I don't care what color you are or where you came from. The fact is, you'll still have to commit to work and work hard with clarity, to achieve your goals and dreams.

And yes, it is that simple.

Defining the Entrepreneur

How do you define an entrepreneur?

Some would say an entrepreneur is a well-financed businessperson, who launches a new business with $20M in venture capital funding. Others would say an entrepreneur is anyone with a great idea and a folding table, a cell phone, and a computer in their garage. Both descriptions might be correct, but that does not really get to the heart of what truly defines the entrepreneur.

I believe what defines the entrepreneur is boldness,

courage, and willingness to accept risk. Brian Tracy, author and business development expert, says "Boldness is a necessary part of courage, but it must be a boldness based on an intelligent assessment of the potential risks and rewards."

Believe me, in today's economic environment it takes toughness and courage to start a business. The most important and necessary characteristic is the courage to step out in the face of uncertainty. Every great venture in the history of man has begun with faith and a giant leap into the unknown.

The only trait that might be common and consistent with successful entrepreneurs and businesspeople is the willingness to take necessary risks. A twelve-year study of successful entrepreneurs conducted by Babson College concluded that the only thing they had in common was the willingness to launch, to step out in faith. It did not matter their age, income, lifestyle, heritage, race, or education. In most cases, the study group had nothing in common except the unique ability to step out in faith into a great unknown without hesitation. Once they had started, *they learned the lessons they needed to succeed.* Many participants in this study surprisingly ended up being quite successful in completely different businesses from where they started.

There are three elements for success for the entrepreneur at play here. The first is *strength of belief* in several areas: the strength of belief in themselves, the strength of belief in their capabilities, the strength of belief in their idea, and finally, their strength of commitment to their decision.

The second element is the entrepreneur's power of flexibility. I've always believed a good definition of an entrepreneur is someone who is passionate about their cause, one who is willing to work at a superhuman pace and can stop on a dime and change directions nearly instantly while updating and adjusting their plan on the fly. While all this is happening, they are still focused and driving forward with purpose. In other words, a successful entrepreneur *must* be flexible.

The third element is entrepreneurial *passion*. To have the ability to take an idea and do what is necessary to build a business around that idea requires a burning, unwavering, whatever-it-takes passion for success. It requires what some call "the Eye of the Tiger!" You can see it in the eyes of entrepreneurs who genuinely believe their business is their mission. And the bottom line is that investors, customers, and employees can see it too. In turn, they can also see the entrepreneur who is going to just give it a casual, half-hearted attempt to see what happens. You can easily pick out the ones who are only partially committed. And the stark reality of it is, if you were an investor, which person would you want to invest in? Would you give money to the one with intense, passionate intention and purpose, or the one who is willing to just give it a try?

In his *Management Success Newsletter*, Brian Tracy says, "Successful executives are those who are continually stretching themselves to move out of the comfort zone, to face the twin fears of failure and rejection and to move forward in spite of them." Today's business environment dictates that there is no place for the faint-hearted and half committed. But if you have an intelligent assessment of the risks and rewards, you have the passion and belief, you're flexible in your plan, and you're willing to step out in faith . . . then you can call yourself an entrepreneur. Remember that to make it as an entrepreneur it's a *requirement* to have the Eye of the Tiger because it is a jungle out there.

Entrepreneurial Lessons from a Mountain Climber: What Kind of Mountain are YOU Climbing?

I have a friend who is a mountain climber. He climbs big mountains . . . big mountains. His name is Mark Carr and he is a successful businessman, Human Resources expert, adventurer, wilderness guide and climber. He has challenged mountains worldwide, such as Mount Everest, Kilimanjaro, The Eiger, The Matterhorn, the Grand Tetons, Mt. McKinley, and many others. When you talk with Mark, you'll soon learn that mountaineering is more than the expected physical challenge—it's also a serious mental and strategic challenge.

One day Mark said, *Big mountain expeditions (like Everest) are a true test of patience and logistics. A typical expedition requires incredible planning involving tons of gear. Imagine feeding up to thirty people three meals a day for six weeks, all above 20,000 feet!* This commentary began what would be a lengthy and fascinating conversation about the relationships between mountaineering and business.

By then, I was hooked. I needed to know more. We soon began to connect some interesting comparisons between building and growing a business as an entrepreneur and climbing mountains. I've compiled a few of Mark's thoughts on the mountain climbing and business connection. Here are excerpts from that discussion.

... "Is this situation impossible or just really, really hard?"

MARK CARR

AUTHOR OF *ASCEND—LEADERSHIP LESSONS AT 28,000 FEET*

On the Mindset of Success

Just as in business, success or failure might begin and end with your mindset. Mark said, "I was climbing on one occasion and my right foot slipped, causing me to swing across the vertical rock wall at 20,000 feet. Smooth rock above, death below. As I settled against the rock wall, I looked up and then down and began to ask myself key questions. Questions like, 'Am I hurt or just hurting?' 'Should I turn back, or should I quit?' 'Is this situation impossible or just really, really hard?' These are the ultimate questions I use during climbs to keep my mindset and focus so I can make key decisions and accurately evaluate if I should turn back or keep going!"

ON FAILURE:

Mark made a powerful point, key to mountaineering and business survival when we discussed the importance of *learning* from failure rather than *suffering* from failure. "We don't value failure enough in our culture," he said. "Failure can be an incredible experience. A lack of 'failure tolerance' stifles people and prevents them from taking necessary risks. It stifles progress and innovation." He went on to say, "I did not make it to the summit of Mt. Everest. I had to turn around less than a quarter of a mile and 1500 feet from the summit. I felt like a failure, but I also understood that it had to be done. If you're smart, you will learn far more from your defeats than you will from your victories."

Learning from failure and learning to not be afraid of it is a great tool. Understanding the value of fear is another great tool. Both keep you focused, awake, alert, and ready for anything. Complacency in business or mountain climbing will kill you!

ON LEADERSHIP:

Mark shared this: "As a leader, you can never expect the people on your team to be willing to endure anything you are not willing to endure yourself. As a climbing leader, I have to tell myself that, yes, this is painful, and it is difficult and uncomfortable. However, I know that I must suck it up and get out there and do what it is I am supposed to do to successfully lead my team and set an example. Leadership is all about feeling like everyone has skin in the game. You want to know that your leader has a sense of shared risk. It builds trust and loyalty among teams when your leadership has as much skin in the game as the rest of your team.

"You will have people who are not as strong as other members of your team. As leaders, if you can help these people find a way to contribute where they feel valuable, you will often get more out of them than you would have if their skills had been on a par with everyone else's skills at the beginning. As a leader on a climbing expedition, it is imperative that you understand your team member's limitations. The 'Peter principle' is alive and well in the mountains, and the impact of people not being aware or ignoring their limitations can be catastrophic and deadly. I believe self-awareness is the single most important factor in successfully climbing a mountain or successfully climbing the corporate ladder."

ON UNDERSTANDING YOUR WHY:

"The meaning of climbing a mountain is in what you bring down with you from the experience on the mountain. This is what counts. If you climb simply for bragging rights, just to say you can do it, that is meaningless. It is not just about standing on top of the summit. If you can make the climb in a way where you are learning and building your leadership skills, helping other people learn, and learning from other people, then that is worthwhile."

ON MEETINGS:

"Climbs involve many, many meetings. The meetings are short and to the point, and need to be effective, where the leader is clear, and the agenda is obvious: who, what, when, where, and how. For climbers, that means objectives, departure times, the route, and equipment. Everyone listens and everyone participates because one missed detail could cost you your life." He goes on to say, "Business meetings should be similar with a clear agenda, defined results, and positive dynamics. The best meetings are the ones where everyone is involved and where the meeting is kept short."

All that Mark talks about here are issues that every entrepreneur faces when starting and building a business. Starting and maintaining a business is not easy. We must make challenging decisions. We must have the discipline, the guts, and the heart to keep at it, make the necessary adjustments, and then get after it again. Or, we must understand when to walk away through honest, ego-free strategic evaluation. Whether you're climbing Mount Everest or building a business, without the proper planning and thought, the consequences are equally harsh. In climbing you could fall to your death and maybe take others with you; in business, you could also lose everything and hurt others around you if you don't have the plan, the discipline, and the faith to make it work.

We were finishing up our conversation and Mark closed with a powerful statement. He said, "Experience alone cannot make up for proper planning, thoughtful risk assessment, and overall preparedness. I have seen experienced people perish in the mountains because they were overconfident in these three areas."

Don't Be Afraid

Mark's comments are uniquely applied to business owners and entrepreneurs. It's a learning experience every day, so whether you're on the mountain or in the boardroom you had better be prepared for anything. Sometimes it's treacherous climbing the entrepreneurial ladder. However, if you can learn to manage the ups with the downs, the result can be very gratifying. I've said it before and I'm saying it again . . . today, right now, is the greatest time in history to be in business for yourself! There are more options available to us every second; more opportunities available for us every day, and more potential inside us than ever before. Now is the time to take chances and do things we never thought possible. For those of us willing to take the leap of faith, the odds are in our favor. One element working for us is simply that so many others have a bad attitude. People are often stuck in the quagmire of uncertainty and have an incredible lack of personal worth, coupled with their fear of the future they perceive. These issues are caused by false perceptions and media-induced fear. Believe me, I see many people losing their businesses just because they are too worried about the "*what ifs*" of the world.

But all this negativity and self-doubt leave more room for those who believe in the possibilities. It's the rare individual who sees the world differently. These are people who somehow fight through the perceived woe of the world and see the same world as one where the glass is ALWAYS half full . . . with promise and opportunity. These people still allow themselves to dream and are among the estimated two percent of our society who have meaningful, written goals. While many cower in fear, there are those who are running the race and getting a massive head start on all the competition. So, when things get better—and history always shows the times will get better—some will just be at the starting line, while others will already be charging ahead.

It's simple, my friends. You are what you think and believe.

If you haven't figured it out yet, life *is* short! We only get one shot at this one, and it's up to each of us to decide exactly how we're going to live the life we've been given. We can be fearful and pessimistic or hopeful and optimistic.

Today IS the greatest time in history to be in business. Step out in courage and have no regrets. Mark Twain once said, "Twenty years from now, you will be more disappointed by the things you didn't do than the ones you did. So, throw off the bowlines, sail away from the safe harbor, catch the trade winds in your sails. Explore. Dream. Discover." Amen brother, amen!

Here's to the Crazy Ones

To me, the word "visionary" is not a word to be taken lightly. To call a person a visionary carries more weight than most words used to describe a person. A visionary is someone who can see what the future could be, then does something about it. They believe in human potential when the rest of the world does not.

When the world lost Steve Jobs to cancer, we lost a true visionary. No matter how movies and books positioned him, he was one of the great minds of our century. He forever changed how we communicate, how we learn, and how we'll see the world for generations to come. In one of my notebooks, I have a quote from Mr. Jobs that I read often. It applies to me. It also applies to many of my clients and friends.

You see, when you strive to be as successful as you can possibly be, when you set goals for the future, when you label yourself an entrepreneur, sometimes that path can be lonely. Sometimes the world sees you as "crazy", a "little out there", and labels you as a fanciful dreamer. If it applies to you, take heart. Here are some words from a guy who lived it and figured it out. And in the end, I think you can say he did pretty well.

"Here's to the crazy ones, the misfits, the rebels, the troublemakers, the round pegs in the square holes . . . the ones who see things differently—they're not fond of rules . . . You can quote them, disagree with them, glorify or vilify them but the only thing you can't do is ignore them because they change things . . . they push the human race forward, and while some may see them as the crazy ones, we see genius, because the ones who are crazy enough to think that they can change the world, are the ones who do." Steve Jobs

Thank you, sir!

How Do You Create Financials for a Startup at the Idea Stage?

I've been a part of many startup businesses and have worked with several inventors and entrepreneurs. Through this experience, I have learned a great lesson. The lesson is about the importance of creating a business plan for every entrepreneurial idea. If you truly believe your idea is a winner, then the idea deserves the thought that goes into creating a business plan. Yes, that's right, a business plan for the idea. And yes, it's a lot of work, but it's the best way I know to force critical thinking about the viability of your idea. It forces you to ask yourself critical questions about all phases of the idea. Sometimes, you will find critical flaws and in others, you'll find new potential.

If you go through the pain of creating a business plan for your idea, it will always prevent more pain later, like the pain of losing all your money because of a half-baked idea. Part of the business plan process is attempting to create a financial section. This is as much of a key exercise as any other part of your business plan. Consider this: literally, with every entrepreneurial endeavor I have ever been a part of, or have consulted or coached for, three things always happen.

And they can be killers.

In almost every case, the entrepreneur misjudges the TIME, EFFORT and MONEY required to be successful. Investors know this. Bankers know this. Smart entrepreneurs know this. Take the time to do a business plan, with well thought-out financial projections, just to save you pain later.

This act forces you to consider every angle and not run out to spend money and time and effort without thinking about it. The process will help you realize the necessary expenses, as well as project your potential and what it will take to get there. But the obvious challenge is always just in coming up with those financial projections for a startup business that is still in the idea stage. So how do you do it?

A quick answer is to know that this is always a *best-guess* scenario. Always! But there are things you can do. First, get a financial template and start by putting in things you know you'll need to consider like rent, office furniture, insurance, utilities, payroll, and such. Again, this should be things you know you must consider whether you start with them or not. A couple of my startups were with a folding table and a telephone and that was it. Those were what are called "bootstrap" businesses. Bare minimums until you sell something. The rest of the financial section is made up with a lot of "what ifs."

I'll do at least three financial projection versions.

1. My "knock it out of the park, emotional, ego-driven" projection

2. My "okay, calm down big guy, let's slow down a bit" version, and then

3. My "holy cow, I didn't plan on that ever happening, *worst-case scenario*" version. This one is based on a clear understanding of what my acceptable minimums would be in my first two years. What I would absolutely have to do to even feel comfortable enough to move forward with the rest of the work necessary to develop and sell my idea. This is just as important to understand as is the Total Success, "knock it out of the park" version.

These projections are usually detailed. This is the kind of pre-implementation and pre-commitment work I always have done to estimate the potential effort necessary. Once again, let me remind you why I am such a jerk about the importance of doing financial projections. I believe that for every business failure I have ever witnessed it was because the owner/entrepreneur had under-estimated the amount of time, money and effort required. Because of this, I always try to do this work and make the extra effort to obtain validation, clarity, and understanding so that if nothing else I'll know exactly what I'm getting into.

This exercise, done properly, can protect your financial future and keep you from losing some hair over time. It takes time—but do it. Have fun with the process. Dig in and really think about all possibilities. Believe me, this kind of planning can save you a lot of pain or, in turn, give you a boost in confidence about the viability of your idea.

How Long Does It Take a Startup to Get Its First Paying Customer?

I am often asked by people who have no idea how a startup works, "How long will it take for me to get my first paying customer?" If you're thinking about this while writing your business plan, good on you. If you're thinking about this after you've kicked off your so-called start-up, then proceed carefully, because more than likely you're already screwed.

To get your first client, you must be prepared and ready to go before you ever hit the streets. A business plan would help, a sales story would help, sales materials would help, knowing how to sell would help. A strong passion and total commitment to your business would certainly help. Heck, a working product would help. It doesn't even have to be completely done yet. And, believe me, there is no chicken-or-the-egg argument here. If your product or service is worthy, if it's a great idea, and you and your team are massively passionate about it, you can sell it before it's complete. I've done it before; it works. You will know when that time is. There is a point in time where you've done enough thinking and planning. There comes a time where you must stop planning, close your eyes, and step out in faith. You can never adjust your plan unless you have launched. I believe there are more steps, but here are eight primary steps you must take to get your first paying customers.

1. **Clarity:** Who is your perfect customer? You must know, or have a good idea at least, who your perfect customer is for your product or service, as it is right now. You should know the gender, age, income, education, favorite sports, size of house they live in, how many dogs they have, what kind of car they drive, are they married, do they have red hair and are they left-handed. You should know everything about them. Then find out where they hang out. Find out where they spend their extra time. Learn how they communicate with each other and how they acquire information. Then, armed with this knowledge, you should NEVER network or dig where they are not. You've got the knowledge, so now it's time to go to work.

2. **Work:** The speed of acquiring a new client depends on how hard you're willing to work. I believe anything short of MASSIVE ACTION is a waste of time. I've done fourteen startups and our goal on all of them was to get money coming in as fast as possible. So, if you're going to call yourself an entrepreneur, you'd better be ready to

work harder than you've ever worked. Scour the country, scour the world, and do whatever it takes to find someone willing to take a chance on your product or service.

3. **Grow a thick skin:** In this process, you will be told NO frequently. You're also going to be told, and in no special order: your product sucks; it's not ready; you're nuts for doing this; I don't like how you part your hair; and so on and so forth. So be ready to wade through the negativity and sarcasm to find someone who gets it.

4. **Learn to sell:** If you can't sell, find someone who can. Now!

5. **Negotiate:** Be ready to negotiate your price. Remember your goal is to sell something now to get revenue coming in the door. So, the question is, "What are you willing to give up to get what you want?" Be ready to make a deal on your first sale or your first few sales. DO NOT be so proud of what you've created that you won't negotiate. You will not survive if you don't. The key to your profit it is to have someone using your product or service and be using it successfully. So, get a deal as soon as you can.

6. **Know what to negotiate:** Let's think about the things you can negotiate. You can negotiate PRICE, of course, and sometimes you must. You can also negotiate certain conditions with the lowering of the price. Some of those conditions to negotiate might be that if you lower your price, the client must give you three leads to other potential users they might know. You might also negotiate, that for a lower price, the new client gives you a guaranteed positive testimonial. You'll need testimonials. Remember, it is not a negotiation unless both sides give something

up. Anything else, you're just providing a lower price and giving up profit.

7. **Be open-minded to change:** I have yet to do a startup where the product or service didn't change, and change quickly, the longer we were selling it. Why, you might ask? Quite simply, the market might like it but sees greater value in it as something else. Sometimes you might find that your product or service might have a bigger and better application in a completely different market than you intended. Just be ready to change. In one of my startups, we found three different applications for our original product that we were smart enough to implement to generate sorely needed capital. Then we went back to the original "big" idea. Keep your eyes open and your ears attuned to what the market says and learn from it instead of sticking to your guns and your ego. Shut up and listen to the market, and the market will tell you how to sell what you have to offer if your product or service is good enough.

8. **Work some more!** Work really, really, really hard! This is the determining factor in how quick you get that first, second, and third client. It might take a week, a month, a year. You must work at it with passion and determination and focus. WORK!

That, my entrepreneurial friends, is how you get your first paying customer.

I Just Look Bald

Hey, hot shot! Yeah, you! So, you think you're a cutting-edge, technologically savvy, app-centric, entrepreneurial businessperson? You've got a degree and you've downloaded every book on the market that has anything to do with business. You know all the hip business terminology, you've bought all the latest technology, you're hanging out with only the hottest apps, and you've tried every "silver bullet" cure-all strategy available today. You're in meetings every day, from sunrise to midnight, and next week you're going to a meditation camp in the desert to get in contact with your past lives, spirit guides, and business muse.

All bases are covered. Check.

You can't lose, right?

Wrong! This is why I don't have hair! I've pulled it all out dealing with businesspeople and entrepreneurs who have been brainwashed to believe in quick-fix, "silver bullet" solutions. We're bombarded daily by personal and business development "experts" who sell and teach that the way to wealth and success is with their magic application/strategy/ approach. It's easy to be sucked into the black hole of an industry that promises instant success.

Now don't get me wrong, some of these ideas and products are good. The problem is that many people will take huge allotments of time, money, and effort to implement a strategy, then discover it doesn't work for them. With no Plan B, they find a new fad and spend all their time and money implementing it . . . and the cycle spins out of control. Again.

I've been blessed and lucky. I've had remarkable mentors. People like Brian Tracy and Zig Ziegler and the writings of Ken Blanchard and Napoleon Hill. Their message is timeless. It is a message of the power in mastering the foundational elements of business success, those steps that have proven to be the foundation of every successful business throughout time.

In my business coaching practice, I preach the gospel of continuous strengthening of individual foundational skills. In fact, weakness in—and an inability to identify, correct and improve weak key elements—is the number one issue that sets apart a struggling business from a thriving business.

Brian Tracy reminded me recently exactly how basic this thinking can be. He told me there are only two purposes of a business: 1) to create value and 2) to generate revenue. That's it and it's that simple. If you don't focus on these two things, you're unemployed.

So, take a deep breath and step back to look at everything you're doing. Ask yourself (and be honest) "How good are my foundational skills?" and "How good are my company's foundational skills?" This applies to things like priority management, goal setting, customer service, sales processes, results tracking and metrics, accountability, financial management, communications, marketing and more.

Look, you can argue with me all you want. I don't care—I don't have any more hair to pull out. The fact is, I've spent nearly forty years in the trenches and learned business from a "street fighting" perspective. Let's get down and dirty. Let's get after it. Some days I won and won big, other days I had my butt handed to me. I always dusted myself off, evaluated what happened, learned from the situation, and moved on. I also learned something else. Successful people the world over, at all levels, shared mostly the same foundational beliefs around creating value and generating revenue.

A few of the many rules I live and teach are:

1. If I master the basics, constantly honing those skills,

I'll always be in the top one percent.

2. I must fail before I can succeed. Any failure is only a failure because I didn't learn something from the situation.

3. The more I work at mastering the basics, the better I become and the more successful I become.

4. Strive for CLARITY in everything!

5. Shut up and listen.

6. I will never stop learning. NEVER . . . ever!

7. The harder I work, the luckier I am.

8. Always, but always, over deliver, and . . .

9. I must always work really, really, really, really, really, hard.

So, if there's still any doubt or opposition to my thoughts left in your mind, if you still want to argue about the importance of mastering the foundational elements of business first, don't sweat it, it's okay, just keep doing what you're doing. That will ensure more opportunity and business for those of us who get it. Those who "get it" are the ones I want to work with and that I believe own the future. Heck, maybe I might be able to grow some hair back.

The 10 Steps to Being a World-Class Entrepreneurial Manager

The first time we ever heard about MBWA was a reference by Tom Peters in his ground-breaking business book, *In Search of Excellence*. Sam Walton of Wal-Mart fame was known to walk stores with a baseball cap on with the initials sewn into the cap. So, what's the big deal? MBWA means Managing by Wandering Around. Peters suggested that most managers only look for employees to be doing something wrong. Most employees are scared to death when they see the boss come down from the ivory tower to walk around. Unfortunately, this attitude creates a management culture that can kill a company, large or small.

The concept suggests that a great manager will work to reverse the "fear factor" and build and nurture an environment where they are on a mission with a different purpose. Rather than instill an environment of fear upon the mere sighting of the manager, the successful entrepreneurial manager is on a mission to find employees doing the right things, good things, productive and profitable things that show their pride of being on the team. The new mission is to look for reasons to praise employees and team members in public. When that happens, when a team member sees the boss coming, they're excited to see them.

If you're an entrepreneurial business owner or manager, it's time to practice MBWA. Here are a few tips on building your "wandering around" skills.

- Appear relaxed as you make your rounds. Employees will reflect your feelings.

- Remain open and responsive to questions and concerns.

- Observe and listen—and let everyone see you do it.

- Make certain your visits are spontaneous and unplanned.

- Talk with employees about their passions, family, hobbies, vacations, or sports.

- Ask for their suggestions on how they might improve operations, products, service, sales, etc.

- Try to spend an equal amount of time in all areas of your organization.

- Catch your employees doing something right and recognize them publicly.

- Convey the image of a coach, not an inspector.

- Encourage your employees to show you how the real work of the company gets done.

Try MBWA in your management and leadership position. The investment in time and money that you spend finding great employees should be equal to your efforts towards keeping them. It is always worth the effort. Team members/ employees will seldom tolerate spending time in a fearful environment, and after a while, they inevitably will find a calmer landscape. The management tactic of looking for screw-ups is archaic and has no relevance in its applicability and value.

So, what do you say? Should we take a walk and look for exceptional employees?

How to Get from Good to Best

My forehead has a bruise on it. The bruise is there because I thumped myself on the head the other night. Why? I had a revelation I should have had long ago. When I realized the importance of this insight, my immediate reaction was to smack myself in the forehead. *Thump*. That left a mark.

The revelation was so obvious. I always try to analyze and understand ways to improve my personal and professional growth. Then, with this knowledge, I apply it and verify it and then even pass it on to my clients. I'm always looking for the basic and simple things that we miss. Sometimes things are powerful and time proven, yet we bypass them because they seem too easy and simple. It is my experience that it's these things that usually have the greatest impact on improvement. Basically, we cannot do the fancy or faddish until we have the rudimentary ingredients of success mastered. Build your foundation, then build the house instead of doing that in reverse.

The revelation was this: we can be good at what we do and do it totally on our own. But we will never be the *absolute best* at the things we do if we don't have a team working with us. When we insist on working solo, it's all about ego that sometimes borders on isolationism. Ego cloaked in stubbornness and fear. Have you ever heard someone say, "I don't need any help, I can do it on my own." Or, "Don't judge me about how I got there, just recognize that I got there!" If we're honest, most of us have not only heard this, but have said it ourselves. If you're a driven, type A personality, you pride yourself on getting the job done and taking all the credit for the results. But the difference between you and the next level of success is that people who level up through using a team is that they get bigger, better, and more lasting results because they use leadership, delegation, and a team of people with the same goal and focus.

The hard fact is, to play in the "BEST" arena you cannot do it all on your own. There is too much to be done, and when you try to do it on your own, you'll find yourself trying to get everything done including low-consequence tasks that it doesn't make sense for you to be doing. The time it takes for you to do these tasks takes time and focus away from achieving the high-value, high-consequence tasks you should be focused on.

The key is to invite and welcome people to share your vision and goal. People who will buy into the results of achieving that goal with you and who will share in the accolades. You are now the team/project leader instead of the sole *doer*. You'll save time, effort and at the same time achieve greater results than ever before. Let's be real. All the bosses, partners and clients care about is that the job is done quickly, efficiently, on time and professionally. So, be smart and use all the resources around you to get these results.

Being the best is a lot easier when you leave your ego at the door and build a team of like-minded achievers looking for a leader. Don't be a success hermit. This approach gives you additional benefits, such as the opportunity to mentor and teach others and to create and build a legacy of leadership that will last for generations. You'll still get the accolades, you'll still make the money, and in the end the result will be a more gratifying success when you bring others along for the ride.

Oh Yes, You Can

Ever heard of the Forty Percent Rule? This nugget says that in most cases people hit a point of mental resistance at only forty percent of their capacity. That's when people quit. I've always said success at almost anything is easy if you just persevere longer than everyone else. In theory, you could use just sixty percent of your personal capacity or potential and still beat almost everyone because they gave up long ago. Does this, in turn, mean those in our midst who are considered geniuses might be that way only because they are putting in more effort, focus, and determination? Could be.

As you face the challenges of life, you really must begin to ask yourself a different set of questions. Questions like, "Am I beat, or am I just giving up?" "Am I hurt, or do I just hurt?" "Is my opponent that much better than me, or am I just not trying?" "Is everyone really that much smarter than me, or have I just quit learning?"

Facts are facts. I am not the smartest person on earth. Yet, I've always excelled at almost everything I've ever done. In some cases, the "smart guys" were working for me. And in most cases I led the herd instead of being a part of the herd simply because I never gave up, I didn't quit, and I truly just outworked everyone else. That is a hard thing for some people to accept. There is a real attitude of entitlement that has infected our current workforce. Many people think the world owes them something; a great job with a big income from the get-go! But, as we all know, the world doesn't care. It doesn't owe anyone a thing. You must *earn* all that you get.

Some people say knowledge is power, but I've always disagreed with that statement. I've said many times that knowledge is NOT power, but the APPLICATION of the knowledge is power. Discipline and effort are real power. Hard work towards reaching goals is power. I am often asked if I have a secret to my success. I sometimes think people who ask believe I carry around a bag of magic pixie dust and when I spread it around people just buy whatever I'm selling. However, when I tell people that I just out-work and outlast everyone else, people look at me like I have a third eye in the middle of my forehead.

To be clear, I am not discounting talent. Talent and skill play an important part of any success, but the world is overwhelmed with underutilized talent and skill. They mean absolutely nothing unless they are put to work.

In 1921 Thomas Edison said, "The reason most people do not recognize an opportunity when they meet it is because it usually goes around wearing overalls and looking like Hard Work." The next time you're ready to quit, give up, or shut down early, remember the Forty-Percent Rule. Just look yourself in the mirror and say, "Oh YES, I can!" I guarantee that you have more energy in the tank, more capacity than you can currently imagine. Be different through extra effort. That, my friends, will be your winning difference.

Go here to get your free checklist for your Start-up Business Evaluation:

businesscoachdan.com/straighttalk

Part
3····

Leadership

Leadership Requires Tenacity and Focus

The pace you set as a leader and the performance standards you demonstrate are key to driving excellence within your organization, especially when you are leading a new company. An astounding ninety percent of all new businesses fail in the first two years, and after that only twenty percent of the remaining businesses thrive. Being one of the few prosperous new businesses requires resilience among leadership—the ability to quickly recover from adversity, whatever it may be. This doesn't imply you will be unaffected by challenges, but it may mean those challenges have less impact on the tasks at hand.

Are people born with resilience? No. Resilience is developed over time by practicing positive responses to challenging circumstances. When you can thrive and achieve a positive outcome for your team despite adverse conditions, you've developed resilience in your role as a leader.

How do you know if you've developed your skills as a resilient leader?

- Are you persistently pursuing goals despite obstacles?

- Do you handle rejection well, listening to criticism from others with objectivity?

- Do you take the initiative to use resources that help you achieve your goals?

- Do you employ problem-solving skills to affect change in your organization?

- Are you flexible, choosing to adapt when necessary?

- Are you personally accountable for managing your attitudes and decisions?

If you manage a team of leaders, do you fully understand each leader's ability to handle the demands of your company? Thriving businesses have a secret. That secret is this: they use powerful personality assessments to evaluate applicants and their existing teams. This information can be the difference between THRIVING versus merely surviving. It's that important. There are several assessments available, so the right assessment can be selected or tailored for your specific needs. In my business coaching practice, we utilize only the proven best assessments available. With these assessments, you now have a powerful tool to better understand the dimensions of superior performance by measuring your future and current leaders against other superior performers. This is powerful, cutting-edge, accurate and affordable.

Tools like this can easily be the difference in long-term success for you and your business, or failure. They can be powerful in not only finding the right person for a job, but also as a way to be sure your entire team is in the right job for them.

Confidence: The True Test of a Leader

If you read the daily newspapers or watch the network or local news, no doubt you sometimes walk away wondering if the world is about to take a dive and come to an end any day now! The economy is tanking (again), more people are looking for work (still), and the government is not functioning at all (as usual).

The SKY IS FALLING, THE SKY IS FALLING!

There are plenty of businesspeople and consumers alike who believe this and live in fear. They manage their businesses thinking the world will end tomorrow and are therefore paralyzed from planning and making necessary bold decisions. Instead, they simply work hard at surviving.

Confidence is the hallmark of success both in business and in life. Confident leaders do not preach, they *do*. They are decisive; they act and inspire others around them. Confidence means taking the initiative and sometimes stepping out in faith, launching into the unknown and taking action. One of my old mentors had a pointed version of a great quote. I repeat it every day. He would say, "The world is full of educated derelicts. They have an immense amount of acquired knowledge. Yet in today's world, knowledge is NOT power. The application of that knowledge is the power!" In other words, you may have knowledge and experience but if you don't apply it, that knowledge and experience is worthless. That, my friend, is how a less educated person who has great work ethic can excel! Isn't that ironic?

When I work with clients, I always get around to explaining a simple fact of life. Applying the knowledge they already have is the key to everything. It is the basis of confidence. Recently, President Michael Crow of Arizona State University made the same point. He was talking at a public function where he urged traditional academics to be roadrunners instead of ostriches. What he meant was that academics tend to behave like ostriches and bury their heads in the sand without using their acquired knowledge to take action and make confident decisions. Instead, he urged them to be roadrunners who move fast and with a plan and, as in the cartoon, outwit the coyote.

Confident leaders learn from past experiences. When faced with tough issues, they know how to make quick decisions and are willing to accept failures and move on. They know how to base their decisions on previous experiences and know that over ninety percent of quick, confident decisions will turn out to be right. Even if you don't know the answer, I would encourage you to make a confident decision, adjust where necessary, and continue to push forward instead of drifting along like a log in turbulent waters.

When faced with a tough challenge and the desire to make a quick, confident decision, follow this simple four-step process. Ask yourself:

1. What happened?

2. Why did it happen?

3. What can I do so it never happens again?

4. Put the solution in place and then move on and make your next confident decision!

Make sure you move with confidence instead of taking the problem or issue to a committee for review. Remember, you need to fail to win.

In his book *Flight Plan*, my mentor, Brian Tracy, compares a pilot and the process for flying from point A to point B with the success process of any business. The *Flight Plan* analogy is a method that will help you reach your end goal. Basically, you must have a plan and you must be confident about the plan. The plan helps you fly into uncharted territory but also helps you steer clear of turbulence, find clarity and purpose, and become a confident leader.

The key to creating your flight plan is to build confidence by taking bold decisions and applying the knowledge you have. Do not wait.

Expected Leadership

In these days of uncertainty, I can tell you one thing I am positively sure of: I am absolutely, positively sure your prospects and clients EXPECT leadership from you. They expect you to be the best at what you do. It's not an apples or oranges kind of thing. If you don't fulfill their expectations, your customers/prospects will find someone else to do the job. Period.

Our prospects and customers are on an ongoing search for their trusted advisor for each of their key products or service needs. From the perspective of a prospective customer, when they choose you as a potential option to receive their business, they expect you to be the expert. Research continually shows that prospects are looking for someone they can feel confident in for everything from lawn care to legal matters. They expect you to know the answers to their questions. They expect you to at least act like you know what you are doing. Gone are the days of just getting by. Gone are the days of having employees with the "I don't know that, I just work here" attitude. That tired attitude will run off a prospect, and when they go, they are usually gone for good.

The aspect of maintaining and protecting your existing customers does not really change that much from what your prospective customer expects. The only real exception is, it's said, more than ninety-five percent of all your existing customers will move to a different provider for minor *perceived* improvements of service and care. More than any other time in history, you must have a strategic plan for how to keep your current customers as loyal as you can, because there is little product or brand loyalty today.

Just remember that a business relationship can go wrong when a business expects their prospects and customers to be the experts instead of assuming that "expected" role themselves. In sales, it's the difference between the "order takers" or what I sometimes call the "commercial visitors" and the product or service sales-solution experts.

The bottom line is this: you can just accept what comes your way, or you can ask questions, gain an understanding of the needs of your clients or prospects from their point of view, and then offer them solutions that make sense. The difference in results can be in the millions of dollars.

The 7 Responsibilities of Business Leadership in Any Economy

I've said it before, and I'll say it again: success has a recipe and don't screw around with the recipe!

The problem for many entrepreneurs and businesspeople is that they try to mess with that recipe and cut corners. You can't cut corners. The recipe of success is foundational and time-tested. It is the foundational principles that I'm always harping on. Mastering the recipe elements and doing the basics before trying anything fancy is the key.

I spoke with the world-renowned business development expert and bestselling author, Mr. Brian Tracy about the foundational recipe of business success. He believes, as I do, that businesspeople and entrepreneurs alike can overcome any economic environment and be wildly successful, through the application of seven categories of business leadership. He stressed that whether international or domestic, the same principles of business leadership and success apply.

Every business owner and entrepreneur must first find

the discipline to focus on these seven business leadership responsibilities before they will ever achieve success, no matter the economic condition.

So, let's look at these *7 Responsibilities of Business Leadership:*

1. **Set and achieve business goals**—What are your goals? Do you even have any? This is the most important foundational rule for business success. Without a clear and concise vision—one that's written down—you will not survive. Key business goal areas include sales goals, income goals, profit goals, cash-flow goals, and margin goals.

2. **Innovation and marketing**—Every company today, no matter its size, should have a single focus on sales. It's quite simple really. You either have enough sales or you don't have enough. Before we continue, let's be sure we understand the difference between marketing and sales. *Marketing* is how you attract qualified leads for your product or service. *Sales* are when you convert those leads and make them customers. Here are foundational questions you should always know the answers to:

   a. What is my conversion rate? How can I convert more?

   b. How can I get bigger sales?

   c. What specifically are my profit margins? How can I get better margins?

   d. What is my customers' frequency of purchase?

   e. Do I have cost controls in place?

   f. Am I being pro-active in my sales efforts or merely

waiting for prospects to call or email me?

3. **Solving problems and making decisions**—A key step in charging forward and finding success or dragging behind and staying stuck or even failing is in how well each businessperson or entrepreneur proactively solves problems and makes decisions. Ask yourself, and be honest, how well do you respond to a crisis? Do you keep calm and focus on a solution or do you form a committee and look for blame?

   Here are specific steps you can take to solve any problem:

   - Define the problem or issue clearly. In other words, *what happened*?

   - What else is the problem? Be sure you identify all issues, one at a time.

   - What is the best possible solution?

   - What other solutions are possible?

   - Make a decision.

   - Act immediately. You cannot wait too long, or the situation will irreversibly affect you. The world, the marketplace, and the consumer simply will not wait for indecision.

   - Continually compare what you gleaned from the decision and be prepared to make changes if necessary.

4. **Set priorities and work on key tasks**—Pareto's Law (the old 80/20 rule) has changed. Harvard research now calls this the 90/10 rule of productivity. This rule says that ten percent of all that we do equals ninety percent of our results, so we must make sure we are always doing the

most important thing at that moment.

5. **Focus on the most valuable use of your time**—The *Law of Three* says that if you make a list of all that you do, there are usually only three things that contribute the greatest value to your business. Ask yourself:

   a. If I could do one thing, and one thing only, to move my business forward today/now, what should it be?

   b. If I could do only two things to move my business forward, what should those things be?

   c. If I could do three, and only three, things to move my business forward, what would those things be?

6. **Set an example and be a role model**—Remember the words of one of my wise mentors: "Someone is always watching." It might be your banker, board member, partner, customer, prospect, or employee. The perception of confidence, self-assuredness, leadership, and passion always creates a powerful perception that everyone sees, whether you know it or not. So, be great in everything you do. Be great in how you walk, talk, smile, stand, sit, because someone is always watching, and they may be important to you at some point in your life and career.

7. **Perform and get results**—Fifty percent of Fortune 500 managers were replaced in three years. Why? Poor performance. The inferior performance occurred because they did not fully understand the results expected of them. Take the initiative and figure out what needs to be done, then get it done. This is key. This is foundational to success. This is the recipe.

The bottom line for business owners, executives, and

entrepreneurs worldwide, is that no matter the economic climate, SUCCESSFUL PEOPLE TAKE ACTION!

Go here to get your Leadership Review:

businesscoachdan.com/straighttalk

Part
4 • • •

Prioritization &
Time Management

Get Your "Time Freak" On

It is well documented: I'm a Time Management Freak. It's my belief that, through the application of foundational prioritization and time management practices, any businessperson, executive or entrepreneur can *double their productivity* in twenty-four hours. Over a year's time this simple practice could be worth a fortune.

I have disciplined myself to planning each coming day the evening before. This, by the way, is a time-honored principle first taught in the legendary book by Napoleon Hill *"Think and Grow Rich"* from 1937. I have set aside at least thirty minutes every evening for over thirty years to list, then prioritize every task I think I need to do the next day. The purpose of this plan is to force me to have the clarity necessary to always do FIRST the most important things I can possibly do to move closer to my goals. No wasted time. No wasted effort.

I never go to bed at night without my "next-day" planning complete. I also teach this process to my clients. In my experience, the number one issue plaguing businesspeople, executives, and entrepreneurs alike is their lack of a task prioritization process and then the time-management discipline to get the high-priority tasks completed.

But prioritization of tasks and managing the time to do them is only part of the equation. Throughout your day, there are *Time Vampires* everywhere. These are the people and things that will suck your business and personal life from you if you allow them to and prevent you from getting the most important things completed.

Managing Priorities and Time in a Virtual Office

How good are you at conducting and managing work from a virtual office? Age might have something to do with just how well you cope. Younger businesspeople have grown up with the concept, but that's not as common for older generations. The fact is, all of us can now work from anywhere in the world with a laptop and great Internet connections. I recall the day when a friend called me, urgently seeking my advice when she heard that the firm, she worked for had decided to close their physical office and have everyone work from home. This was a shocker for my friend, who had been with the company for fifteen years and always loved her morning latte, gossip with her co-workers, and got a great start by wishing her boss a fine good morning.

The decision came sooner than expected when the firm announced their decision to sell off the physical space, cash in on a booming real estate market, and add the profits to the company's coffers. So, everyone in the ten-employee business now had to work from home. She fretted about working on Skype, co-workers in pajamas, and a virtual life.

For any knowledgeable worker, this is the new norm. Got talent? Sell your skills from anywhere. My first advice to you, if you intend to start working virtually, is to set up an environment that will help you discipline yourself to do great work. Working virtually offers several advantages, including the absence of rush hour traffic, better productivity, and of course some tax deductions. Set up your virtual office in an area of your home that is free from distractions and consider it a sacred place for you to do serious work.

Next, make your office purchase good technology for

you. By this, I mean computers that connect to the Internet and phones that allow you to be heard clearly. If your firm is scrimping on technology, be clear about how this will impact your productivity and will not allow you to collaborate with workers in a shared environment. Each day define clearly what you plan to do and set expectations with your co-workers as well. This will make them feel involved and through your efforts of providing clarity, they will understand when and how to seek help. Once your goals for the day are defined and you know what tasks to accomplish, collaboration in a virtual world is simple and straightforward. Tools like ZOOM and Skype enable us to see each other, share desktops, edit content, and share ideas in ways that we could never have imagined a few years ago. Many tools are free and are designed to enhance your productivity. Take some time to play around with these tools and I guarantee you will soon be an expert.

Another powerful consideration deals with the positive and negative aspects of working in a virtual environment. I'm sure you'd all have heard what Marissa Mayer, the CEO of Yahoo! did when she took over the helm of the company. She stopped telecommuting for a lot of tech workers and asked them to come to their offices. This was because a lot of them were doing projects remotely, but not collaborating well.

Remember, the greatest disservice to your employer is to misuse the trust they have given to you when asking you to work in a virtual environment. So, be ethical, keep your time sheet and do great work. Taking your dog on a walk, or looking at your Facebook, Pinterest, or Instagram during office hours, will lead to missed deadlines and sloppy work. One day, you *will* get caught and this can ruin your career and your life. Remember, the most positive aspect of working in a virtual office is to have the opportunity to create your own workplace and determine your destiny by doing fabulous work.

Finally, please don't try to be the 24x7 virtual office worker. Call it a day when your work is done and shut down your computer as you would do in a physical space owned by your employer. This will help you keep your sanity. When the workday is over, by focus on family issues and the personal time you need to rest, relax, and unwind.

Too Much Free Time?

If you find yourself with too much free time, there are only two things that can be happening. One, it's intentional. You're either a bum or you won the lottery and don't have to work if you don't want to. Or, two, you don't have any goals or personal vision. A famous friend of mine used to say that the great thing about climbing mountains (achieving goals) was that once you achieved the summit, you could always see another peak to climb.

The Japanese have a word, *kaizan*, which means, "continuous and never-ending improvement." Adapt that word and live it. If your vision is so short that you truly run out of things to do in a day, you need to sit down and take some time to reset your future. Think about what you want to do and how you want to do it. If you are working, figure out how to contribute more, add value, smash your quotas. If you don't have a regular job anymore, then think about what legacy you want to leave and how you will do that. Is there a charity you could get excited about? Where might you volunteer your time and make a difference in someone's life?

Just don't waste your time. Don't let your life circle the drain while you watch.

Here's an interesting exercise that I ask my clients to do from time to time: I ask them to write their own eulogy or obituary. I challenge them to think about and then write what they hope people would say about them when the time comes. Will they say, "Here lies a great guy who worked too much." Or, do you hope people will say something completely different? Are you doing anything today to ensure what people say about you when you're gone will be something, you'd be proud of? What kind of legacy are you building today through the examples you set?

Writing your own eulogy is a hard subject to tackle, so I'm going to ask you to do something much more fun. This is part of an exercise I do with clients working on one of the phases of goal setting. So, get a piece of paper and then simply allow yourself to dream. Some of us have forgotten how to dream because of all the limitations we've put upon ourselves over the years. I ask clients, "How big will you allow yourself to dream, if you know, without a doubt, that you will not, cannot fail?"

Even if it's not your nature to dream, go ahead and do it. Write down your dreams, everything you can think of. What are your personal goals, hopes and desires? Be open, be honest, and dream without restrictions or constraints. Write everything down that you can, then stop to look at what you have on your list. You might be surprised. Don't be shy. Go ahead and dream. I won't tell anyone.

Do You Know You're Wasting Time?

The answer to this question isn't easy! You can usually tell, though, if you're in fact, wasting time, based on how you feel at the end of the day. When you finally conclude your day, do you catch yourself questioning whether you accomplished anything at all that day? Do you find yourself saying, "I was busy all day, but it feels like I didn't get anything done."

If you're saying that or even thinking that, it's a sure bet that you wasted a ton of time. And, here's the thing about time, you can't get a wasted year, month, week, day, hour, or minute back. Time is perishable. Once it's gone, it's gone. So, do you treat the time you have like a precious coin or like dispensable garbage? Using the coin analogy, the question now becomes, *Are you in charge of spending your precious coin, or do you give it to someone or something else?* In other words, are you in control of your time?

Three questions you can continually ask yourself during the day to begin to think differently about time are:

- Today, was I really busy, or really productive?

- Is what I'm busy at, REACTIVE or PROACTIVE? In other words, am I spending my time reacting to things, issues, stimulus, and other people's needs, or am I taking charge, understanding what is important, then disciplining myself to be proactive and get the important things done first?

- A powerful mantra to ask yourself every twenty minutes at first is: "Is what I'm doing right now the most important thing I can possibly be doing right now to move my goals forward?"

It's important to understand that mastering time takes an immense amount of focus and discipline. Here are the basics, to get started:

1. **Manage priorities first, not time.** You must learn to prioritize all that you do, focusing only on the highest priority items. These are tasks that have the biggest consequence if you don't do them. Find the #1 highest consequence task and do it first, followed by the second highest consequence task and so on. Once this list is complete, then manage the time around accomplishing the highest priority tasks, first. You'll soon learn that nothing else matters other than completing the high-priority tasks. In my business coaching practice, when I do this exercise with clients as many as eighty percent or more of the tasks people think they need to do, disappear. Poof! They're just not important anymore.

2. **Plan the night before.** Napoleon Hill wrote in the business classic, *Think and Grow Rich*, in 1928, that the key to success was prioritizing your tasks to attack and complete the night before. The Law of Attraction is then engaged and working for you. Instead of waking up and wondering about what you're going to do (or react to) today, you clearly know the most important tasks you will focus on and complete. In most cases, that gives you a two-hour or more jump on any competition. It's powerful.

3. **Have clear goals.** If you don't have clear goals for your work or your life, stop everything and get some. Whatever you need to do, clear, concise, written goals are crucial. Knowing what you want in business and life goes a long way towards helping you evaluate your priorities.

4. **Action Exercise.** Get yourself a yellow pad and write down, right now, all the tasks that you think you need to do tomorrow. Now ask yourself which ones have a consequence and which ones don't. Eliminate the ones that clearly have no value to your job, career, or life. Now, prioritize one task that has the highest value and the highest consequence . . . then that is your first and only project tomorrow. Start with it and work on it until it's done.

Look, with the time we have, it only makes sense to do our best to spend the precious coins of time the most beneficial way possible. If what you're doing now isn't working and you know that it isn't working, do something about it. Otherwise, time and life will simply slip away before you know it and all you can then do is *wish* that you would have invested your time differently.

Know No!

Here's what you need to know about the word NO. One of the great truths in life is that the word "no" can be a complete sentence. Simple, quick, and easy. Learn to use it. "NO!" can be your friend. Billionaire, Warren Buffet said, "The difference between successful people and VERY successful people is that very successful people say NO to almost everything."

Some leadership experts will tell you that one of the recognized traits of great leaders is the ability to know when to say no. So, with that in mind, let's call this ability to say *no* a skill. In turn, a skill is something that can be learned. Think how it might change your life if you learned to be comfortable saying no. I will guarantee, that no matter what you do for a living, you can double your productivity by learning to say no. It's easy to say. Sometimes it's no more than a grunt and a side-to-side head shake, and you'll get the point across.

How many interruptions a day do you allow that could be solved simply by learning the skill of saying *no*? How many times do we allow someone to drop by for a chat? How many times do we get sucked into a conversation that turns into petty griping, complaining, or mindless chatter? I call the people who do this Time Vampires, as they exist to just suck the energy and positive attitude from a person. But this all could have been avoided just by you saying, "No, I'm busy with an important task right now."

How many times do we accept meetings without knowing anything about the purpose of the meeting? Your life can change simply by avoiding the dreaded M.A.S. or Mindless Acceptance Syndrome by just saying, "No, I need more information."

What makes this act so hard? Sometimes interruptions can be malicious, simply one person taking advantage of the other because they know that the other person can't say no. Or, sometimes people think that by saying no, they will hurt the other person's feelings—and of course no one wants to upset anyone else, right? So, people tend to agree to things, to allow interruptions, and buy things they don't want or don't need just because they can't, or won't, say no.

When the "very successful people" that Warren Buffet speaks of use the word *no*, what they're really saying is, "Look, you didn't give me enough information for me to say yes. If you want to sell me anything you need to ask me some questions and give me pertinent information. Then, and only then, might I say yes, but until then . . . no."

Know that "no" is a clear, concise, complete sentence and is a verbal and strategic skill you can learn. It's also one of those things in life that you need to learn, because it's rarely taught. When you learn the ease and simplicity of rejecting what doesn't serve you, you'll be astounded at how quickly your life also becomes easier.

Managing the Noise

The time we have every day is precious. Your time should be a positive force in your life, but for far too many of us, time and how we use it becomes a source of stress, the cause of excuses, frustration, and may even lead to procrastination or anger. Some tell-tell signs you're having problems with time management include constantly putting things off, rushing at the very last minute to get things done, and becoming exhausted in the process. The problem is that we allow the noise of life to get in the way. We allow low priority noise to take precedent over high-priority, clear, crisp issues. The key to personal success is to learn to manage the noise that steals our time.

You *can* take charge of your life today. You'll need to commit to change and more importantly, adopt a powerful discipline. My favorite definition of a discipline is "Doing what you have to do, when you have to do it . . . whether you want to or not!"

Productive discipline is required on a daily, minute-b-minute basis if you truly want to once again control your time and manage the noise. David Allen, the author of *Getting Things Done* says "The problem is that everybody is getting distracted by the latest and loudest. They fail because they haven't captured, clarified, organized, or built in a regular review system they trust."

To get your new system started, let's keep it simple. There are four initial disciplines to master.

1. **Honest analysis:** Okay, it's time to be brutally honest with yourself. Are you fed up with the way things are going? If you are, quit making excuses and do something about it. Sit down and focus on analyzing the way you spend a typical day or a typical week. What are the things you need to do more of, and do sooner, to improve the quality and quantity of your output and results?

2. **Planning:** Plan your next day every night before going to bed. Every evening make time to sit down in silence and list *everything* you need to do tomorrow.

3. **Prioritization:** Once the list is complete, ask yourself which one of your tasks has the highest consequence if you don't do it. Be honest. Not everything has the same consequence. Whichever task has the highest consequence, that's the one you do first. Follow this by number two and so on. You may be surprised at the things that have little consequence but are getting in the way of things that have a huge consequence. A simple Law of Time Management is "Never allow the most important things to be at the mercy of the least important tasks." When you get up in the morning, you are ready to do the most important task of the day when you are the most rested and least distracted.

4. **Personal accountability:** Ask yourself every thirty minutes throughout the day the one primary question that will keep you on track: "Is what I'm doing right now

the number one thing I should be doing to move my goals ahead?" If what you're doing doesn't fit this criterion, STOP doing it and get back on track.

You can improve the quality of your life TODAY by committing to controlling your time and managing the noise!

Go here for additional guidance
on task prioritization and management:

businesscoachdan.com/straighttalk

Part 5 · · · · · · ·

Crucial Sales Development: For You or Your Team

Open for Business

Just to be clear . . . I'm OPEN FOR BUSINESS!

I'm not quite so sure about how that fits with the mentality of many business owners today. There are a lot of mixed signals out there. When you go shopping (for anything), do you sometimes get the feeling that the businessperson you're dealing with doesn't really want your business? Sometimes it feels like they've given up, they expect to be closed in a month, they're struggling to break even, the government is out to get them, blah, blah, blah. Sometimes it feels like they're saying to me, "You don't really want to do business with me today . . . do you?"

I want to make my feelings absolutely, positively, and completely clear:

I believe that this is absolutely the greatest time in history to be in business!

And I am, without a doubt, OPEN FOR BUSINESS! So, allow me to share with you just what that means to me and what it should mean for you!

What I do isn't always right for everyone, but I, at least, want the chance to find out! You should put this same kind of laser-focused attention on your client to discover their needs.

One key to retaining clients is to help them be successful based on how they define success, not by your pre-determined definition of success. To understand anyone else's definition of success, you have to look them in the eye and listen to their needs and then collaborate with them to solve those needs. I know listening to the prospect or customer is a lost art in American business, but I promise you that's what you need to do if you want people's business. It is the only way anyone can truly know what the client wants and in turn for you to know if you can efficiently and powerfully deliver the results they want. If you can't tell the client exactly what you'll do, you can't expect to earn their business.

It's hard work. Then you must work even harder to keep a client's business because customer loyalty is not an easy thing to earn or keep today. This is where you go that extra mile to simply meet their expectations. You must not only *meet* their expectations for being cared about, but you must *exceed* their expectations. In fact, it goes beyond even that. To earn business and keep it for months and years to come, you must work hard to *amaze* the client with the highest level of customer care. That translates to customer satisfaction.

People have lots of choices today and with the ever-expanding capabilities of technology, the future is sometimes unbelievable. Yet nothing replaces honest hard work, experience, hope, passion, support, positive attitude and one-on-one accountability. I'll put that up against technology any day.

So, what do you say? Let's do some business!

How Many Cold Calls Should a Top-Notch Salesperson Make in a Day?

How many cold calls should a top-notch salesperson make in a day? This, my friends, is a question that I often get while coaching a *struggling* sales organization. Ten years ago, even five years or less ago, the answer might have been different, but today, the answer is easy. NONE! Do not waste your time making cold calls. Unless you're a telemarketer or working a boiler room of some sort, the cold call is not an effective tool in today's marketplace. There's just no place for it. The concept is archaic. This is particularly important to know if you're a "top notch" salesperson. The market has outgrown the need for cold calling. In fact, the act is seen by most prospects now as unwanted and unnecessary. In the past, cold calling was accepted and even welcomed by many business owners, but that has changed. It has changed because business owners have access to instant information, at their fingertips twenty-four hours a day, through many different forms of communication devices. If they want to know about a product or service, they can Google it!

So, in short, there are three issues that all "top notch" salespeople already know.

1. **Cold-calling is a terrible waste of one's time.** It's random and prospects today hate random. It's intrusive, and, intrusive in today's world is unwelcome, unwanted, and unnecessary. And the sales focus is usually TELLING the prospect something (i.e. *"I'd like to tell you all the reasons you should buy my product or service."*). The simple fact is that today, no one wants to be told anything. You'll burn a ton of valuable time "smiling and dialing" or "hot knocking" hoping to find someone who will talk with you.

2. **Be extremely clear about who your #1 prospect is, then target them.** Focus your time on acquiring referrals for your specific target customer. I always suggest that you look for three key groups.

   a. The first group are those people who know you or think they know you, who like you, trust you, and, hopefully, want to help you.

b. The second group is people who know people that you need to know.

c. The third group is people who could be strategic partners. These are people who have the same target customer as you have, but if that customer bought from the both of you the money would come from different budget buckets.

3. **Stop with the pitch, ask more questions, shut up, then listen.** Top salespeople listen more than they talk. If you find your perfect target prospect, remember that your conversation, from the beginning, isn't about telling them all about you, your company or why they should buy. If you can't tie a prospect's *need* to a clear and tangible deliverable, the prospect simply does not care. Their attitude becomes, whether they say it or not, "SO WHAT?" If you can take the time to clearly understand the customers' needs from the customers' point of view, you are royally screwed. The prospect is more interested in WHY you do what you do than how you do what you do. You, in turn, should be interested enough to ask a few strategic questions. And those strategic questions do not include, "Tell me about your business!" Because they know, and you know, you should have already researched that information. You're wasting their time if that's where you start and your odds of having them buy something immediately go down. In fact, they're probably beginning to think of ways to get rid of you.

Start with these three foundational thoughts and adjust how you go about becoming a top-notch salesperson.

Let's Dance!

I almost got shot the other day! One of my clients called to tell me about a successful meeting they had just completed, which ended in them getting an important new customer. This was a really tough, hard-fought win. We had worked intensely together to create a powerful and strategic plan to use in the coming meeting . . . and the plan worked!

I received the call while I was driving, and I got so excited for my client that I began cheering and honking my car horn. Evidently the gentleman driving next to me could not understand my sudden and unbridled excitement for my clients' success and because of his lack of understanding, mistakenly assumed I was honking at him, which, based on his reaction, was a direct affront to his family's good name or something like that.

Anyway, he began yelling at me.

I couldn't make out what he was saying, thank goodness. He was also making some strong gestures of which I'm sure was foreign sign language that he expected me to understand. So, as anyone would do, I did what I thought was most prudent. I turned into the next most accessible neighborhood I could find. Luckily, he didn't follow.

My point, dear friends, is that it is important, no, necessary, for you to celebrate your wins and the wins of others every day of the year. You literally need to look for the opportunities and reasons to celebrate in business and life. I don't care how small the win, you MUST celebrate! Make it a point to do a companywide "happy dance" when something good happens to you, an employee, a partner, a spouse, children, or friends. If they can't do it for themselves, do it for them. But we need to celebrate more.

Sam Walton, the genius behind Wal-Mart, made it a point of management style and company culture to actively find employees doing something RIGHT, to literally watch for them doing something over and above the so-called "call of duty." His reasoning was simple. Most other business-management cultures are based on catching people doing something wrong or incorrectly. Come on, admit it, that's the way it is. If the boss is coming your way, what is your first reaction? To go hide, right? However, in reverse, if you constantly praise and celebrate as a matter of culture, when it does come time and is necessary to reprimand, then that is the exception rather than the norm.

This strategy and attitude is applicable across the board as far as I'm concerned. It's just as right for large companies as it is for small companies. So, make it a point to celebrate every time you, an employee or your spouse or children turn hard work into success.

Make it a point to find reasons to celebrate.

With all the things that make business ownership or management a challenge today, it's up to the owner, the leadership, the manager, or the salesperson to step up and do something that's easy, and just simply, something that is the *right* thing to do. Let's celebrate individual and team success every day of the year.

Come on people, let's dance!

Selling: Adjust or Fail!

There are changes taking place in how and why you are successful (or not) in selling just about anything. It's a subtle change, one that kind of creeps up on you, like losing hair the older you get. One day you have it and the next, you don't.

But it is happening, and it is pervasive. It can be something that you understand and learn, and then adjust and take advantage of, or instead, you can wake up some day and feel like you've just been sucker punched.

The fact is, we have technology to blame. Like it or not, it's a fire-breathing monster that simply can't and won't be stopped. It's moving fast and continues to pick up speed. There is no way to avoid technology and all it has to offer. My eighty-seven-year-old mother had a smartphone, or shall I say she demanded a smart phone.

So, technology is changing consumers in a big way, and again, if you're in business and you sell anything, you had better be adjusting how you do business or you will lose, and you will lose badly.

Here's just one of the adjustments you must make.

According to new research from BIA/Kelsey Group, ninety-seven percent of all consumers are now researching products and future purchases online. Ninety-seven percent.

Some of the latest e-commerce statistics show there's no slowing. This is not a trend; it is the future of business. It's here now and will continue to evolve.

- Global retail e-commerce sales exceeded $2.43 trillion in 2017 and is growing nearly twenty percent a year with no slow down expected.

- Seventy-one percent of all shoppers believe they will get a better deal online than in stores

- Eighty percent of the online population has purchased something using the internet

- Consumers no longer rely on only one resource for information. On average, consumers are looking at 7.9 different sources for product information. In addition, and to put a cherry on top, the *Online Retail Payments Forecast* found that nearly seventy percent of consumers are "comfortable" shopping online with credit cards.

And yet:

> Seventy-four percent of small business websites do not sell online and don't have an e-commerce-enabled website.

One final report stated what I believe is the real danger/opportunity within all these numbers: nearly seventy percent of all consumers will have made a buying decision prior to the first face-to-face contact with your business.

So, what really does all this mean?

It means that potentially your consumer has made a complete 180-degree turn in how they think and whether they buy from you or someone else. I believe we all need to look at our consumers/shoppers with a completely different eye. The facts are, that when a consumer/shopper calls you or walks in your door, you need to understand that they will seldom just be shopping. Today, when they walk in your door, they have already done their research on what they want and who might be the best provider of those goods and services. They know who has "made the cut". They have done their research, online, on their own time frame and have evaluated their options and narrowed down who THEY CHOOSE to do business with.

When they call or walk through your door, you need to understand they're not going to want to get your "pitch." They don't want a grocery list of all your features and benefits, and they don't need you to tell them anything. They want you to LISTEN and ask questions and answer their questions. Not only that, but more than likely, they will now be buying for emotional reasons. They've done their diligence online, they've done their bottom-line research, and compared features and pricing. It's important that you understand this has happened when they walk in the door or call.

Their next step is the key. Now they want to justify their decision with emotion. Do they like you? Do they trust you? Do they feel like you care about their needs or do they think you only think of them as a commission check and a sale?

Whether you get their business or not will be determined by the level that you understand this shift in consumer thinking.

Are you ready to sell them . . . now?

The Basics of Selling Anything

If you've followed me for a while, you know I'm a staunch believer in mastering the foundational skills of your profession before you try any fancy stuff. This is true in the profession of selling. The industry overall tries to make selling much harder than it really is. If you stagger through all the books and webinars and seminars on how to do sales, many, if not most, are based on teaching or telling you about a new "silver bullet" sales technique, emerging fad, or strategy. I believe before you can fire that amazing "silver bullet" you must have a gun that works. The gun, of course, being the foundational skills required to be able to implement the new strategy.

A few foundational skills are necessary. Those include

prospecting skills, basic communication, persuasion, negotiation, and presentation skills, writing skills, marketing skills, plus a strong work ethic, and many, many more!

So, let's keep it simple and break down the four primary elements to selling anything.

Find a prospect with a problem or need that you know you can solve. Look, contrary to many so-called networking experts, you don't need to go to massive events and collect thousands and thousands of business card leads to find someone to sell your product or service to. You just need a few, specific leads with people who have an immediate need that you are a specialist in solving or helping people with. Don't spend your time trying to convince someone why they need you. Find someone who is actively looking for someone like you to help them with their need.

Make sure the prospect really wants to solve their problem and it is high on their priority list. You can't force a prospect to hire you to help them solve a need or problem that they don't think is a big deal. Again, rather than make that decision for them, get your prospect to tell you about what their needs are. Ask some questions, then, just shut up and listen. Any prospect will tell you how to sell them . . . I guarantee that!

Now, show them how you can help solve their need better than anyone else. What can you do that is unique, special, and collaborative, compared to any other option? What is it that you offer that sets you apart? What do you do and say that will give your prospect the HOPE that you can help them improve their business and their life?

Work with them to solve the issue or need. Dig in and work hard with your new client. Work with a passion and desire to honestly help them. Work as a team and continue to give them hope. With this, you now become a trusted advisor, and that translates to a long-term relationship. Why? Because you have now become a valuable resource.

The fact is, if you master these four foundational elements of selling, it's all you need. Everything else is simply a waste of time for both the prospect and you!

The 18 Disciplines of Selling—Part 1

I am a sales professional. It's what I know, it's what I've studied. Learning to be a world class sales professional is the source of my greatest successes and failures. It's all I've done for most of my life. My profession is that of a business coach. Yet I consider myself a sales professional applying my skills to the field of Business Coaching. It still surprises me when I hear people still turn up their nose or act fearful when I tell them they are salespeople.

"Oh, I could never be a salesperson!"

"I don't want to be a salesperson!"

If you've ever sold an idea to your kids or a teacher, you've sold something. If you've ever asked for a raise, you've sold something.

The ability to be a good salesperson is not as hard as most people make it. There are tons of books that discuss every phase and level of selling. Every strategy and nuance. However, it's hard to find something that really covers the basics. The "daily" elements and attitudes it takes to be a good salesperson. In fact, I believe the hardest thing to master to become a great salesperson is simply the art of committing to a daily discipline to master and then do the basics, day in day out. Renowned business development guru, Brian Tracy, defines discipline as "Doing what you need to do, when you need to do it, every day, whether you want to or not!"

Here are what I believe are the 18 Disciplines of Selling that you must master daily to be a consistent and highly compensated sales producer, whatever you are selling. But before we get into the disciplines, there are some rules to this game.

Rule 1: A good friend and colleague of mine once said: "When you wrestle with a gorilla, you don't quit when *YOU* get tired . . . you quit when the GORILLA gets tired." The Zen Master of Minnesota

In other words, you must work hard at whatever you're doing and selling. You must develop a thick skin and a laser focus and let nothing get in your way. You must never give up.

Rule 2: Understand that THERE ARE NO SHORTCUTS TO ANY PLACE WORTH GOING! Once they learn the foundational principles, many people then disregard them and move on, looking for a silver bullet. There are no silver bullets in selling. Learn the craft and do not leave the path.

Rule 3: If sales are the way that you choose to make a living, remember:

- If you're not selling, you had better be in front of a customer or prospect

- If you're not in front of a customer or prospect, you had better be selling!

- Driving, planning, meetings, thinking, eating, and talking on the phone DO NOT COUNT! Only face-to-face and belly-to-belly with a customer or prospect counts in selling.

Rule 4: Selling happens in a series of steps. These steps can happen quickly, or over time. Successful selling occurs only when you EARN THE RIGHT to take each step.

- We must SELL a prospect on talking with us

- We must SELL (earn the right) to ask them questions, then to ask personal questions

- We must SELL them on what we offer

- We must SELL them on the value of the offering compared to SELL needs

- We must SELL them on liking and trusting us

- We must SELL them on committing to us

- We must SELL them on the continuing and on-going value of our product or service

- We should ALWAYS be selling!

So, let's define selling. Selling is "the PROCESS of helping a person conclude that your product or service is of greater value to them than the price you are asking. Your prospect/customer MUST feel they will be better off because of the transaction than they would be without it."

For your prospect/customer to buy, they MUST be convinced that your service is:

- The best choice available, based upon their needs, and

- There is no better choice for them to spend the equivalent amount of money

Selling is convincing your prospect or customer of this

and getting them to commit.

Quite simply, if we don't SELL, we DON'T have customers. Without customers, we don't have a business. The elements of successful selling are not hard. Again, the hardest part is having the discipline to apply the fundamental elements of successful selling daily. The FOOTPRINTS OF SUCCESS have already been laid. We just need the discipline to do the basic elements of sales success every day. It's about mastering the little stuff, that makes a successful salesperson, no matter what you're selling!

The 18 Disciplines of Selling—Part 2

In *The 18 Disciplines of Selling—Part 1,* we began by discussing the rules of the game. So now let's talk about excelling at the "game" of selling. In Part 2 of the *18 Disciplines of Selling,* we're going to discuss disciplines #1 through #3. You'll notice quickly that each is separate, but connected, and believe me it's the little things that contribute most to great success.

Selling Discipline 1:
Be proud of what you're selling and what you're doing.

You'll make a lot of sales simply based on how your prospects *perceive* how confident you are. When I coach businesspeople to success, the first thing we talk about is the perception that your prospects and customers will develop that helps them decide whether they want to work with you or buy anything from you. This is based totally about the "vibe" they get from watching how you walk, talk, act, smile, listen and think. If you are going to be successful at selling coaching, you must "Walk like a coach; talk like a coach; act like a coach; smile like a coach . . ." Or said in another way, "Walk like a professional; talk like a professional; act, smile, listen and think like a pro." When you walk into a room you want people to say, "I don't know what he/she sells or does, but I want some of it!" Simply put, a prospect or customer does not want (particularly in today's economy) to invest their hard-earned money in someone they don't believe in. You wouldn't want to work with a heart surgeon who says he "thinks" he can do a great job with your surgery, do you? So even if you're new at a job or profession, you must act proud and confident and committed to what you're doing, because, if you're not, the customer or prospect can smell it from a mile away.

Selling Discipline 2:
Act like a leader and winner.

Sales success is an attitude with the purpose of creating a powerful perception of success. It's a look and feel, and that's something you need to remember from the time you wake up to the time you go to bed. Your customers and prospects, and just as important, future customers and prospects, will be attracted to you simply due to your positive attitude. In these times of bad news and uncertainty, prospects and customers WANT to work with someone who they perceive as knowing more about an issue or need they have than they do. So, you as a salesperson, no matter what it is that you're selling, MUST act like a leader and winner and the person your customers and prospects and future customers and prospects are looking for. Hold your head up high, smile, act confident (even if you're not as confident as you could be), walk straight and speak with authority. Prospects are looking for someone with solutions and a positive outlook. Remember, SOMEONE IS ALWAYS WATCHING! It may be a prospect, a customer, a competitor, a board member, an investor, or a vendor that's watching, but count on it . . . someone IS always watching. So, set yourself apart by being perceived as a leader and winner, now.

Selling Discipline 3:
Expect success and never give up.

When asked how he felt about all the failures he had while inventing the light bulb, Thomas Edison said, "I have not failed. I've just found 10,000 ways that won't work." To be in business today, you must simply expect success. No matter how bad it gets or how bleak it looks, you MUST expect a positive outcome. The only thing that is sure other than death and taxes is that YOU WILL FAIL, and YOU WILL MAKE MISTAKES. It's how you deal with the failure and the inevitable mistakes that will dictate your future in sales and business. The founder of IBM, Thomas Watson once was asked by a young employee, what advice he would give about how to speed up their rate of success and he quickly said, "You must increase your rate of failure."

We will make mistakes and screw things up from time to time, but that's simply a fact of life. We must be dedicated to learning from a mistake, take a moment to decide how to prevent the mistake from happening again, then put it in the rear-view mirror and move forward. For others to have enough confidence in you and your product to buy something from you, they must believe in you and what you represent. If you expect success, it shows . . . if you expect failure, it shows as well. By thinking positive thoughts and never giving up, you overcome all the bugaboos of selling: call reluctance, fear of rejection, cold calling and more. You want to exude the attitude that "I have a great product and I won't give up because I believe in it so much." Anything less, and you represent the old joke about the downtrodden sales rep whose body language alone said, "You don't want to buy anything from me today . . . do you?"

Zig Ziglar once said, "You were born to win, but to be a winner you must Plan to win, prepare to win, and expect to win!" Nothing else needs to be said.

The 18 Disciplines of Selling—Part 3

Selling Discipline #4:
Be PASSIONATE about what you're doing and let it show.

With all my clients, the first three disciplines are foundational. Our first three disciplines are based on being proud of what you're doing, then acting like a winner and leader, followed by expecting success and never giving up. But, none of it works unless you're *passionate* about what you're doing and show it. Now don't panic. I don't mean the fake smile and actions, jumping around and such. What I do mean is finding that burning fire in your gut to accomplish your goals and letting people see it in your eyes, in your speech, and your actions. When you make a statement about your product or service, let your prospect hear it from your heart. Again, it's a perception that is established. Every prospect would, I guarantee, *rather work with someone that they perceive is committed to getting the job done* than someone with a perceived lackluster attitude or focus. Let them see your confidence and positive attitude. That is, again, something that will give you the slightest edge and sometimes that's all we need.

Selling Discipline #5:
Get yourself organized.

Don't even try to argue with me here! I've yet to see a highly successful and consistently successful salesperson who is disorganized. In fact, the issue of disorganization may be the number one, biggest excuse for lack of activity or failure, that I've seen. Research has proven this time and time again and business development experts have written hundreds if not thousands of books on the subject, and they all say that, psychologically, personal disorganization leads to cluttered thinking, which in turn leads to a distinct lack of focused productivity. So, NO MORE EXCUSES. Get organized. Take the time to do it, because it's not that hard. Simply remember the primary rule for organization: Never touch a piece of paper unless you do something with it. Here's your shopping list: one box of Avery labels, one box of file folders, one box of green hanging files. Now, here's the drill: Push everything on your desk onto the floor. That's right, you heard what I said! Now pick everything up, a piece at a time. Determine what the subject is, and if it's worth keeping, and if it is, get a label and write the proper heading on it. Put the label on the folder and put the folder in a hanging file. Do that until you're done. Now you have a system. The hardest part of this is being tough and committed enough to have the discipline to do this every day. So how tough are you? Follow the system, and if you do, your productivity, your sales, and your profits WILL go up. Act today.

Selling Discipline #6:
Set clear, concise, and written goals.

Okay, I know what you're saying: "Yeah, yeah, yeah, I've heard that before. Everyone says that. I've got some but they're in my head." Well pal, that's not good enough. By most accounts, and the numbers vary, seventy percent of our society does not have any goals whatsoever. Another twenty-eight percent has goals of some kind and only two percent or so have written goals. But here's the kicker. Many business development experts and some noted research say that the two percent to three percent with written goals control over ninety percent of all income. This is a fact that has been touted for over half a century. It might be worth your time to review your thinking here. It's hard to establish proper written goals. You must push yourself and be honest with yourself about what you want and what you need to improve on. For some, that's a huge task. There are countless books fully dedicated to goal setting. Most systems are similar, so find one and do it now. You must get started on it now! The foundational rules for goal setting are all the same. They are based on the acronym of SMART goals.

S is for Specific. You must have a clear and concise vision.

M is for Measurable. You must know where your starting point to clearly see your results.

A is for Aligned with your values. You cannot set goals that go against your value system.

R is for Realistic. Your goals must be attainable, yet must make you stretch to achieve them. and

T is for Time-bound. You must establish a reasonable time frame to achieve your goals.

Jim Rohn, the world-renowned business philosopher once said, "Success is neither magical nor mysterious. Success is the natural consequence of consistently applying fundamentals." And that my friends are what the Eighteen Disciplines are all about.

The 18 Disciplines of Selling—Part 4

My personal commitment is to believe that no matter how long you've been selling you must have a continuous mastery of the skills necessary to remain efficient and to ensure long term success. We last discussed Disciplines #4 through #6. In Part 4 we're going to discuss disciplines #7 through #11.

Selling Discipline #7:
Have a daily prioritized plan. How do you plan your day?

Do you get up in the morning, go to work and sit at your desk and say, "What do I need to do today? I sure hope I don't forget anything?" If you do, you're not alone. In my business coaching practice, I'm continually shocked and surprised at how many people are in the same boat and I guarantee you their results are mediocre at best. The people who are making the big money and who are always successful, begin each day a daily plan of action they have prepared in advance, usually the night before each new business day. Success psychologists and experts have proven in testing that if you plan out your priorities and tasks for the next day the night before, your "super conscious" mind will work on the opportunities throughout the night and have you ready to go the next morning. In Napoleon Hill's groundbreaking book, *Think and Grow Rich*, he calls this a result of your "infinite Intelligence." Once you notify it of your plan, it will help you achieve your plan by bringing to bear all that is necessary for you to be successful. With a plan made the evening before, when you get up the next morning, you walk to your desk and pick up your written plan for the day. You're instantly ready to go and you instantly have more than a two-hour head start on most of your competitors.

Be sure your day's plan is prioritized as well. Ask yourself, "What is the most important single thing I should be doing, right now, to move my goals forward?" Another way to say it is "What can I, and only I do, that if done well, will advance my business and personal goals?" Then, to stay on track, adjust the mantra and pause during the day to say, "STOP, am I doing the most important task I could possibly be doing, right now, to move my goals forward?" If you're not, stop and refocus.

Selling Discipline #8:
Have a clear understanding of who your
ideal target customer is.

This is a simple concept most businesspeople today have never fully considered. In today's market, you CANNOT sell to everyone. Pareto's Law is in effect more than ever in today's business place, but with a change. The law says that eighty percent of all your results will come from twenty percent of your activity. In this case, eighty percent of your sales will come from twenty percent of your customer base. But today, many business development experts will tell you that it's narrowed even further to the ninety percent - ten percent rule. That is, as much as ninety percent of your results will come from ten percent of your activities, customers, etc. With the impact of the internet and the expansion of options for today's consumers, you have no choice but to identify your ten percent and focus on them. Who are they and what do they want? This, by the way, is one of the key "business killers" I see every day in my coaching practice.

Businesspeople continue to target everyone, versus the key customer, that true customer who delivers the lion's share of business for them. You had better find out who your primary ten percent is and quick, because how you take care of them, service them, and cater to their needs, may just represent the life or death of your business.

Selling Discipline #9:
CLEARLY understand your Unique Selling Proposition (USP).
It may sound crazy, but you can easily do the research. Most top business development experts will confirm that what is estimated to be over ninety-five percent or more of all salespeople/businesspeople cannot tell you just what it is that they do in under ten seconds, or even under thirty seconds for that matter. Try it out. Ask a salesperson, any salesperson. Heck, ask yourself! Surprised?

I hear it all the time as a business coach and I test it all the time. Rarely can the businesspeople I talk to tell me concisely and with clarity what it is exactly that they do. In many cases, my prospects and clients, once they understand the concept, are shocked about their complete lack of clarity and inability to voice this precisely. Many are honestly surprised they've been able to stay in business as long as they have with such a lack of clarity. In our coaching sessions I show them how they can clearly understand what they do and, even more clearly, what is it exactly that they do for a customer. It's just far too easy to say, "I sell real estate" or "I sell cars." Take the time to sit down and really think about what is unique about what you do, how you do it and, why you do it. That's what prospects and customers want to know. Otherwise, they will always ask that one inevitable and frankly logical question. "So, what? I don't care. I don't understand, what's in it for me?"

Selling Discipline #10:
Create a powerful ten-second and forty-second marketing message.

Ditch the Elevator Pitch. The Elevator Pitch is dead. The Elevator Pitch is all about telling a prospect all the reasons why they should buy something from you. Guess what? They don't care. Nobody wants to be told anything today. They don't have to be told; they have Google. So, if you're telling instead of asking, you'll be out of business. Most consumers today (and never forget that you're a consumer too) will say to themselves, "SO WHAT?" when you give them a general statement about what it is that you do or why you do it. If you're a realtor, understand that there are thousands and thousands of other real estate people in your market, so why should your prospect/customer use you instead of ANY of the others? That's always the real question, isn't it? The salesperson who can answer the SO WHAT question is the one who will win every time. Take the time to truly understand *why you do what you* do for your prospect or customer and be able to say that in a ten-second statement. After this, you can then tell them *how you do what you do* for them in the more traditional forty -second statement. Practice your statement by sitting down and listening to yourself say it and ask yourself the SO WHAT question, then be sure your statement has an answer. Tell the prospect why you do what you do and what's in it for them to hire you or do business with you. With this kind of clarity for yourself and your prospect or customer, your sales will improve in a matter of days.

Selling Discipline #11:
Talk to lots of people and ask lots of them to buy.

Okay, too simple right? However, you would be amazed at how many salespeople mistakenly think that a little bit of activity is something that will get results. IT JUST DOESN'T WORK THAT WAY! Sales, at best, and at absolutely any level, is a game of numbers. The more target prospects you talk to, the more opportunities you'll have to find the ones ready to buy . . . now! Discipline yourself to talk to as many target prospects as possible every day and every week. This should be part of your goal system. Every action that you take, every conversation, should be focused on finding someone who might be your client. In today's market, a salesperson simply cannot afford the time to develop a large group of prospects. Developing long-term prospects should be a limited part of your day, but the bulk of your day should be looking for the low-hanging fruit. Remember the four S's: Some WILL, Some WON'T, So WHAT, Someone's WAITING! But also remember this.

The 18 Disciplines of Selling—Part 5: The Finale

I believe in having a system anyone can follow. One of these systems is the 18 Disciplines of Selling. We have covered the skills necessary for selling with Disciplines #7 through #11. In Part 5 we'll finish with disciplines #12 through #18.

Selling Discipline #12:
Be consistently persistent.

Once you find a prospect who's interested and willing to take the necessary steps to be your customer, NEVER let them off the hook. Be consistently persistent in everything you do. It doesn't matter what you're selling, from financial services, to insurance, to business coaching. Most salespeople quit too early, either through fear, assumptions, or sheer laziness. Fear, in that you're just afraid to go out and look for customers. Assumptions are ones where you're making decisions for your customer and judging how they will react before you even speak to them. Today time is your enemy and you cannot be the *conscience* of your prospect. Never get into the mindset of "I'll call them back next week." or "If I call them back this week, they'll think I'm bugging them." It's not your job to guess what they're thinking, it's your job to sell them your goods and services. Here are the facts:

- 48% of all salespeople NEVER follow up with a prospect
- 25% of all salespeople make a second contact and stop
- 12% of all salespeople only make three contacts and stop
- Only 10% of all salespeople make more than three contacts

Here is the bottom line:

- 2% of all sales are made on the first contact
- 3% of all sales are made on the second contact
- 5% of all sales are made on the third contact
- 10% of all sales are made on the fourth contact
- 80% of all sales are made on the fifth to twelfth contact

So, if the prospect is in your target audience and they've

given you the buying signs, stick with them. Odds are, your competitors won't.

Selling Discipline #13:
Understand the Customers' needs from the Customers point of view.

In other words, become a master of the art of listening. Ask your prospect and customer lots of questions, then shut up and listen. If you can master this simple, act an amazing thing happens. Your prospect or customer will tell you how to sell them! Few people today listen to anyone else. That, my friends, is a killer for people who sell. If you're perceived as being a bad, inattentive listener, you're perceived as not caring. If you become the one salesperson who does listen, then your prospect or customer will tell you things about their business and themselves that will earn you the right to do business with them. Then you simply satisfy their *needs* (not always problems) from a unique perspective. You satisfy their *needs* from their point of view, which makes the solution remarkably powerful.

Selling Discipline #14:
Close early and often.

What's so hard about asking a prospect to buy? Or asking a customer to buy more? Understand that closing is NOT a big event. Closing a sale is incidental. If you've earned the right to get to this point by asking questions and listening, if you've tied your USP to the prospect's specific and exact needs, then you have earned the right to simply, casually, and logically ask them to buy. It should just make sense as a natural progression. The problem is that many salespeople do the work, but many also never ask the prospect to buy. When this happens it's the first salesperson who walks through the door with a similar, logical solution that gets the order.

Selling Discipline #15:
Understand clearly what you're willing to give up to get what you want.

It's the first rule of negotiation. There's negotiation in every selling situation. You negotiate with your kids, friends, parents, relatives, potential employers, employers, and of course business prospects and customers. So be prepared. Don't walk into any situation without clearly knowing what it is that you are willing to give up to get the deal. Is it price? Is it time? Is it scheduling or payment terms? Whatever it is, know what you're willing to give up before you ever get into a situation that could cost you money. You can build your conversations around this knowledge, just as you can build your presentations around this knowledge, just as you can build your presentations around this knowledge. When you clearly know what you're willing to bend on, then you instantly have the upper hand in the deal and can then move to an ideal win/win situation.

Selling Discipline #16:
Track everything.

Every truly successful salesperson can tell you their KPIs (Key Performance Indicators) and where they currently are in relation to them. This begins with goals that are clear and precise. With some simple charts and graphs you can track the goal and your progress, daily, weekly, monthly, quarterly, and yearly. It's imperative. As the wise man once said, "How do you know where you're going if you don't know where you're at?"

Selling Discipline #17:
Work really, really, really, really, really, really hard.
Don't listen to some of the new age blather that says if you just clearly understand what you want, then you can simply sit down, and wish for it, and it will happen.

It just doesn't happen that way.

Yes, you must clearly understand what you want in your life (goals), but once you know, you must work for it and work hard. Especially in sales, your report card comes out every week. If you want to earn more, go out and sell more. Planning, goal setting, working the phone, working prospects, networking, marketing, workshops, and sales calls all take time, effort, and planning. Nothing replaces hard work. Nothing! I'm often asked why I've been so successful as a business coach. It really comes down to the basics. The same people who ask me that question are the same ones who won't believe me when I tell them I work the Disciplines of Selling every day. But it's true. I had a call last month where we went through this scenario. The bottom line was that this fellow had conducted over the course of a year about fifty closing presentations. In the same year's period, I had done 186. That was my "secret." I had conducted nearly four times more selling presentations where I asked people to buy something. Because of this, my odds were just higher than his of finding a prospect to say yes.

Selling Discipline #18:
Repeat Discipline 17.
Once again, nothing replaces hard work and focused effort. What you put into a task is what you will get out of the effort, so get to it!

This is the bottom line that I offer to all my clients and workshop attendees, and literally every prospective client I've ever had. There are three things I know to be true:

1. This is the best time in history to be in business and be in sales.

2. This is the best time in history to maximize your potential, whatever level you're at.

And, if you're passionate about the success of your prospects or customers, and it shows, they will buy whatever you have and will work with you a very long time.

> ## Go here for your client acquisition checklist:
> **businesscoachdan.com/straighttalk**

Part
6 • • •

Negotiation

Business + Life = Negotiation

It was 7:00 a.m. and I was on the first leg of a business coaching trip, on a plane going . . . somewhere. And, I'm in my usual early morning going-somewhere fog because it's too early (for me anyway) to get into my travel/work mode because I need coffee! Lots of coffee! My goal is to write a great blog for the coming week. So, I'm slogging through a file of random magazines and articles I've saved to read on a trip just like this one. I'm looking for inspiration from someplace, anyplace, but am still unfocused enough to not really care.

For some reason, however, a headline in a full-page advertisement in an in-flight magazine jumped off the page and made contact with my awakening "lizard" brain. Here was a picture of a beautiful woman smiling at *me* while she was smoking a huge cigar. Now I found this to be quite interesting. Having spent several years in the advertising and marketing business myself, I'm quite sure this particular ad was the idea of some highly paid and revered Madison Avenue marketing genius/ advertising geek, and that the ad itself had probably won lots of awards while not actually producing any results for the client. I was sure of this because the ad copy below this exotic picture had absolutely nothing to do with the picture of the lady and the cigar!

The copy below the image could have easily stood on its own. It said: "In business, you don't get what you deserve, you get what you negotiate."

Something began to wiggle and flutter in my mind. Negotiation is the answer. It's a major contributor to the secret of success. Whether they know it or not, everyone negotiates. *Business IS negotiation. Life IS negotiation*! It was as if a light radiated from the page and an invisible laser beam sprung forth and radiated directly between my eyes. This had me intrigued, excited, buzzed . . . and awake.

I'm suddenly on an inspired writing jog with my new muse. My total focus is on that ad copy. I'm inspired by the lady and the big cigar.

This must be like the elation Hemmingway and Steinbeck felt while writing their classics. The "force" was now with me. The words flowed effortlessly. One blog spilled onto my tablet, then two, then three. The coffee kept coming . . . one cup, two cups . . . five cups. How much time passed, I'm not sure. An outline for future workshops on negotiation appeared. A presentation title peeked around the corners of my brain: "Practical Application of Negotiation Principles."

Brilliant, I thought. Then an interruption in the force occurred. My muse became blocked as a distant voice told me to stop what I was doing and prepare for landing. The flight attendant stared right at me. "But I'm on a roll," I say. "I can't be stopped, not now!"

The attendant looked at me over the top of her glasses, just like my fifth-grade teacher, Mrs. Gile did, and she said, in one of those fifth-grade teacher voices, "Sorry, there's no negotiating on this."

How ironic.

The lady with the cigar seemed to smile.

The gist of the matter is that while on an early morning business flight I had an epiphany. It wasn't just an old run-of-the-mill epiphany, oh no, it was an Old Testament, waters parting, head spinning kind of "aha" moment epiphany. Looking back, I think this was probably an advertisement for a negotiation seminar or software or something like that, perhaps. I might have known if I would have looked on the previous page, but the page I was looking at said nothing about any product, so my mind ran with it.

When you think about it, that's a powerfully simple yet exacting headline. It's magnificently elegant yet refined. Gads, that rolled off the tongue a little too easily didn't it? Magnificently elegant yet refined. Wow! Anyway, it's all about the headline and what it means.

We all, at some point, will go to the store to buy something. Canned soup, socks, pickles, clothing, shoes, appliances, carpet maybe. We go in to buy these items and we walk up and pay for them, just like that. We accept the price, we nod, and we pay. Done!

In turn, how many times have you tried to sell something that might include a product or service or asked for a raise at work? Or maybe you tried to get your kids to do something . . . and ended up settling for the easiest solution.

We should always remember that most of the time, the price or the "deal" is negotiable. A price on any goods and/or service is almost never a number that's scientifically derived. It's just a number someone hopes to get for the goods or service. You don't have to believe me. In almost any of the great books on negotiation by Gary Karrass or Herb Cohen or any other authority on the subject, you'll find a similar thought on how prices are derived. Think about it. There is the famous Manufacturer's Suggested Retail Price (MSRP) and then there is the sale price. There is a deal the seller would like and a deal they would gladly accept. Have you ever wondered why everything always seems to be on sale? If not this week, it will be on sale next week. Putting things on sale is a business's way of negotiating the price or deal for you. If you won't try to negotiate with them, they'll do it for you, but on their own terms. They'll win either way!

So, here's the kicker. If you follow the advice of the experts, you should at least try to negotiate because *everything is negotiable*. At this point I must throw out the yellow caution flag. Be careful and be sure to pick your battles. It's unlikely that the next time you go grocery shopping you'll want to try to negotiate the price of ketchup. The store won't like it and your fellow shoppers in the checkout line will probably throw you out of the store before the store throws you out. But when it comes to business dealings, be sure the thought of negotiating is top of mind.

All I ask is that you always set aside a moment to think about negotiating. It's a tough business climate out there and if there is a chance that you might get a better deal, and everyone is still happy, then you owe it to yourself, and you owe it to your business, to negotiate. Never forget that the world owes you nothing. Very few of us are heirs to fortunes or are entitled to anything, so to get more out of business and life than just surviving, to truly thrive, never forget the immortal words of the lady with the cigar: "In business you don't get what you deserve, you get what you negotiate."

The Laws of Negotiation

I have realized, at this point, the simple premise the "lady with the cigar" has come to represent. Basically, she was teaching me that we must negotiate all phases of business in order to simply run with the pack or even be ahead of it a bit, and that we must, as always, keep it simple.

Just as with any skill, it could take years upon years of study and practical experience to become a cutting-edge, hard-core, world-class negotiator. When you really get into the science of negotiation, it can easily become just that—a science. Mastering of the art of negotiation is a challenging strategic, psychological, and scientific discipline.

However, if you're like me, you really don't' have the time or inclination to do that. So, I'll practice what I preach in my business coaching sessions. I believe we try to make everything harder than necessary by not practicing the Law of Simplicity. The Law states that "In everything that we learn and do, we should try to first purely and clearly understand the most basic elements of the issue." In this basic simplicity, we can learn and adapt the foundational principles and then apply them with greater intensity and within a more immediate time frame.

So, what I'm about to give you are some thoughts on negotiation that puts the key "rules" of the game into a simple and, more importantly, applicable language. First, let's have a clear understanding of what the word negotiation means. In the simplest terms, the word negotiation means "The process of achieving agreement through discussion." Also, remember that when negotiating with customers, prospects, suppliers, family, friends, or others that it is not always the best price that is the objective, instead, it's how BOTH of you can be successful.

One of the most commonly asked questions that I get concerns when a negotiation really begins. My answer is always the same: the negotiation begins at the point that you begin talking. It is part of your entire process. But also remember that IT'S JUST A GAME. Don't take it personally—it's not personal—so have some fun with it. It's not life or death, it's just trying to get something more from the agreement.

There are four results, and only four results from any negotiation:

I WIN—YOU LOSE: I'm happy, you're not so happy

I LOSE—YOU WIN: You're happy, I'm not so happy

I LOSE—YOU LOSE: Neither one of us is happy over the deal but we did a deal anyway

I WIN—YOU WIN: Everyone is happy over the deal and will probably do more deals in the future!

Win-win is the result that we'll call the foundational rule. If it's not a win-win deal, it shouldn't be a deal.

Before we get to the RULES of NEGOTIATION there are a few LAWS of NEGOTIATION that we must mention:

First Law of Negotiation

Never enter a negotiation with a short timeline. If you're negotiating with the restriction of a looming deadline, you will usually lose.

Second Law of Negotiation

Never negotiate on an emotional issue or out of emotion. Try to take emotion out of the equation. If you can't, you'll usually lose. I once met a world-class negotiator who had for years been involved in negotiating peace agreements between nations. He told me that when it came time to negotiate for a new car, he always took his neighbor with him to help because he was too emotionally close to the issue.

Third Law of Negotiation

Plan on taking your time. Never negotiate on anything that you think you must have right away. Set yourself a time frame that you'll be okay with in getting the item or situation bought or achieved. When you do that, you have the most powerful tool available to you in any negotiation—the willingness and ability to walk away from any deal and potentially find what you want somewhere else.

I would have never imagined that a simple innocuous advertisement in an in-flight magazine on an early morning flight would have created the explosion of thought and words that it has. But it seems that my new creative muse that has been with me for the last couple of weeks has, alas, taken us to this final phase of our renewed clarity on the power and importance of NEGOTIATION in our everyday personal and business life.

We've concluded this process with these basic uncomplicated RULES OF NEGOTIATION that I believe are all that you'll need in order to get more out of life and for your business. Yes, there are more rules and the more sophisticated you get, the more complicated these rules become. But these are the everyday foundational rules that will get you going, keep you going, and will always hold strong in any situation.

So, here are the 8 Basic Rules of Negotiation.

The 8 Rules of Negotiation

Rule 1: **Always know who has the authority**—It's this simple: do not ever, and I mean ever, negotiate with someone who does not have the authority to make the deal. Be sure you're dealing with someone who has sign-off authority. Otherwise, you're just wasting time. An old mentor once explained it this way: "Never take a 'no' from someone who can't say 'yes.'"

Rule 2: **Understand what you're willing to give up to get what you want**—Try to think the conversation through. Do as much research and diligence as you possibly can before you begin. Know what's the most you might pay or what might be the maximum time you might wait. Know precisely what you will and won't do. Know precisely what it is that you want out of this coming conversation.

Rule 3: **If you are asked to give something up, BOTH SIDES must give something up or it's not a negotiation**—Everything in this process is reciprocal. You should not be the only one giving in during a negotiation of any kind. For instance, you might say, "I'll pay your price if you'll deliver it free." Always ask for something in return.

Rule 4: Price ISN'T the only issue in a negotiation— Remember, it's not always about price. Most people will lower their price or ask for a better price simply because that's what everyone does. So, if price isn't necessarily your issue, you'll certainly take a lower price if someone is willing to give it, right? In fact, issues on the table in the early stage of negotiating usually aren't really the major issue up for negotiation. Usually, if not always, there's a greater issue that's really the main issue and leads us to the next rule.

Rule 5: **He who has the most information is always in control**—Again, do your homework. Know everything you can possibly know about what it is that you want and about who you're negotiating with. Other than spending some focused time with selective online searches it's important to simply shut up and ask lots of questions. Our brain processes words at 500 to 600 words per minute. You can talk at a rate of 150 words per minute. So, shut up and process. LISTEN! Understand your opponent's needs from their point of view and then help them achieve those needs.

Rule 6: **Negotiate the little things first**—Always get an agreement as early as possible. Some call that "breaking the ice." Get something positive going by building agreement and trust and remember you might need to GIVE to GET.

Rule 7: **Be strong and have nerves of steel**—Once you get to that point where you have told yourself that you won't go any further, then you must have the guts to hold firm on that position. Be confident about your position and stick to it if you can justify it.

Rule 8: **Know your exit strategy**—Never, never, ever be afraid to walk away from any deal. That's the key, and it's a powerful tool. You must know in advance where that point will be when you know you can no longer achieve a deal or when the other side cannot be trusted. Remember, it's just a game and the goal is win/win. If you don't feel that's the kind of deal you have, smile, then walk away. If you can't get the deal you want, there are other places and people who will work with you.

It's a hard world to do business in, and you're not going

to simply get handed anything in business or life. No matter how hard you work, or care, or try, you must understand that the world owes you nothing. So, in the end, the lady with the cigar really had more to say to me than just an unconnected advertising message. She helped me truly understand that "In business AND life you don't get what you deserve, you get what you negotiate!"

I swear she winked at me! Really, she winked.

Go here for your Grass Roots Negotiation Tips:

businesscoachdan.com/straighttalk

Part
7

Creating a Business That Thrives

Building a Business Success Team

Whether in sports or big business, every success story is always a success story for a team. The accolades may go to an individual who persevered mightily, who fought against the odds, who toiled beyond belief, but seldom did they not have a winning team behind them. They always have an "A" team of technicians, advisors, mentors, friends, parents, and spouses. If you dig long enough and deep enough, you'll always find those who contributed to the individual's success. Bill Gates once said his key to success was to hire people smarter than he was. But in today's world, you don't have to be a Hall of Fame sports star or a titan of industry to surround yourself with smart people who can and will coach, train and mentor you to business success. You can build your own team of superstars to guide you. They're often not on your payroll—most of us couldn't afford them. But they are available to anyone and many times at little to no cost. They are professionals whom we can work with to help us in those strategic areas of business in which we have no expertise.

Oh my, what did he just say?

Yes, I said, "in areas we have no expertise." Now is not the time to play Business Superman. Too many businesses go out of business today simply because the owner tried to run all areas of their business on their own. Drop the ego That's not only impossible, it's stupid. There are experts in specific and strategic fields that you can recruit into your team. Some critical areas of expertise I recommend everyone acquires: a qualified business coach (of course); an accountant, legal advice, marketing expertise, sales consulting, banking, and financial counseling. In fact, I find that a great financial advisor/counselor is an essential team member and a key player in planning the future of a business. A good one can do much more than just put your money in the market, they can help you lay a smart plan that will take you from cradle to grave. The following is a checklist of some of the essential elements I have my customers look for in a great (not just good) financial advisor. They include:

1. Look for an advisor who will focus on recommending a plan that will **reduce your risk while building wealth.**

2. Look for an advisor who will make every attempt to *understand your specific business and personal financial planning needs—FROM YOUR POINT OF VIEW.* In other words, they're great listeners.

3. Look and listen for an advisor who is truly **service focused.** You want to know that once the plan is complete you WILL see them again at least once a quarter.

4. Look for an advisor who is **truly qualified.** What is their background? What is their success record? Who makes up the bulk of their clientele? Is it successful customers who have been with them a long time or do they have an average customer retention of less than a year?

5. Look for an advisor who is both **creative and innovative.** Many advisors today are merely sales focused and are pushing specific financial products. They're more interested in selling you a product than fitting products and strategies to your individual needs.

The bottom line is that a GREAT financial advisor is an essential voice in both your business and on your personal success team. Now is not the time, nor are we in the economic climate to go it alone. I believe you can be one of the business success stories in the next decade simply by creating your SUCCESS team as soon as possible.

Planning for Success: Clarity in Your Business

The number one reason businesses fail today is a distinct lack of clarity in all things concerning their business. In today's market, we often see businesspeople who have been in business twenty years or more who will fail due to a lack of clarity about their business or about marketing their business. If you haven't noticed, how we conduct business is changing drastically almost daily and it will continue to change. New options, new technology, smarter customers, and an uncertain economic environment all contribute to this tsunami of change.

To accomplish effective planning, it is essential to have total and complete clarity about all facets of your business. Oh, you can plan, but if your plan is based on old and uninformed thinking, then how effective will the plan really be? As the old axiom goes, "Have you been in business twenty years, or, one year twenty times?"

I have a little more than fifty key "clarity" questions I always focus on with my clients. The challenge for most people going through these questions is that they have never answered these sorts of questions honestly. It's not that they're purposefully lying but that they simply have always given the *easy* answer rather than the *right* answer. I encourage people to dig deep and be honest. The only way for this exercise to work is to really think about the question. Ask yourself if you really do know the right answer. If not, do some research and, perhaps, just open your eyes. Talk to your employees and talk to your customers and, more importantly, talk to your prospects. Understand who they are and what they need *from their point of view*. Then you will have the clarity to be able to (maybe for the first time) tell them who you are in a clear and concise manner. Here are a few of the questions I ask:

1. **What business is your company in?** One of the greatest blocks to a business's growth is the lack of clarity regarding the true business in which it is engaged. If you don't believe me, do this simple test. Conduct a fifteen-second exercise and ask your employees, friends, or associates what business they think you're in. You *will* be surprised at the answers you get. Keep in mind that the true business you're in is really what your business does for your customers from an emotional standpoint. The classic example is of the railroad industry. Everything changed when the industry discovered they weren't in the *railroad* business, they were in the *transportation* business. Another good example is real estate. Are you in the real estate business? Or, are you the person who helps families make the best choice in the biggest financial decision they might ever make? There's a big difference.

2. **What is the core competency of your company?** A business only succeeds to the degree to which it is aware of, and capitalizes on, its core competency. So, what *one* thing does your company do better than anything else? Are you featuring that competency and taking advantage of it?

3. **What is your core product or service?** You had better have complete and total clarity in what products or services are paying the bills and which one aren't. Apply Pareto's

Law here. You might know it as the 80/20 rule. Which twenty percent of your products are giving you eighty percent of the revenue? Many researchers now say due to the impact of competition, the internet, and economic changes, the rule is now the 90/10 rule. Whichever you choose to work with, you should know what people want and what they don't want. Run the numbers and get rid of products and services that don't sell, then focus your business and your time on the ones that do.

4. **Who is your core or ideal customer?** Based on your answer to the 90/10 rule exercise, who buys those products and services? What do they look like? What is their age, income, family status, wants, needs, desires, and what are their hopes and fears? This is an essential point of clarity. Many businesses have all their marketing efforts and dollars targeted at an audience they think or assume is their audience, yet after some research, they realize this group simply is not their customer base after all, and with that revelation, they realize their marketing dollars are wasted.

5. **What does your ideal customer consider of value?** Don't guess here. You had better be doing some research. Talk to your customers and prospects. Do some simple surveys and understand what they want from *their* point of view. Is it price or quality? Is it service or on-time delivery? Simply put, the worst enemy of any relationship is unmet expectations. So, understand what your customers and prospects want and expect . . . then make the changes necessary and deliver what they want.

6. **Who is your core competition?** The question isn't

always who the competition is, but today, *what* is the competition? Is your competition really the obvious competition? Take a second look and understand this point of clarity. Sometimes your biggest competition is not another business, but many times it is the internet, for instance. If you don't have a presence there, then everyone who sells your products or services on the internet *is* your competition.

We just discussed the first six questions you need to ask yourself. Let's look at the others you must ask.

Take your time and answer these questions and challenge yourself with each step. More than likely, patterns will begin to occur and hopefully, you'll have some major "aha" moments.

7. **Who are the core people in your company?** Identify your keepers. If you have problem team members or slackers, now is not the time to have anyone on your team who isn't a major contributor. Deal with it. An old mentor once told me, "Always work with and try to change the person. And, if you can't change the person . . . change the person."

8. **What are your core sales and marketing methods?** Millions of advertising dollars are being wasted today because "That's the way we've always done it." Marketing effectiveness has changed, and your consumers have changed. If you're not getting results, stop the strategy you're using and build a new strategy that works. Be flexible enough to change and change quickly. It could mean life and death for your business.

9. **Ask yourself,** "What can I do NOW to protect my core business from the worst thing that could possibly happen?" A key component of surviving and thriving is preparedness. It's tough but you must ask yourself what is the worst thing that could happen to your business? Be aware and then plan to prevent it from happening or at least how you would deal with it.

10. **What are the core strengths** that I have as a person? Leaders always know:

    a. What they're good at

    b. What they're bad at

    c. What they like to do

    d. What they don't like to do

11. **What are my core opportunities?** Open your eyes and understand what opportunities are staring you in the face. Be aware of them and don't miss them, act on them now. The market and your customers and prospects will not wait on you to figure out what to do.

12. **What is your core and unique selling proposition?** In today's world, differentiation is the key and if you don't know why someone should buy your product or service over that of any competitor, then you simply don't deserve to be in business. We must know, clearly and without a doubt what your specific uniqueness is.

I have a friend who is smart and a marketing expert to boot who says, "It's not just a selling proposition. It's not just something that's compelling. It's all about something that is *unique* and one of a kind—which your business should be."

There are several questions you can ask yourself, but a couple of the most important are:

a. Why would your ideal customer buy from you instead of your competition?

b. Why would your ideal customer buy from your competition instead of from you?

This is where we, many times, will fall back into the easy answers. People will buy from us instead of the competition because "we've been in business for thirty years." or, "because we have the best people." That might have worked in the past, but today people will turn around and walk out your door when they hear these empty and easy remarks. Most businesspeople have no idea how easily they can be replaced, but replacing them is as easy as doing a Google search. If you have been honest with yourself as you go through these clarity exercises, you might find your Unique Value Propositions begin to emerge. Write your wisdom nuggets down and begin to hone them for use in your marketing materials and your sales messages.

Once this is done, you must apply the ultimate test. These two questions can potentially make or break your business totally based on how honest you were with your answers. All value proposition statements must pass the test of these two questions. This applies to anything you say about your business in press materials, marketing materials, sales pitches, and more. Simply train yourself to step back and look at any statement you are making and apply these questions. These are questions you must envision your prospects and customers asking themselves anytime they read or hear anything about your business or products.

The questions are:

a. **So what?**

b. **W.I.I.F.M.** (What's in it for me?)

Create visuals in your head of a customer or prospect with a big neon sign attached to them. Imagine that anytime you say anything to them about your business, the sign lights up and begins blinking with the words "So What? What's in it for me? So What? What's in it for me?"

After you train yourself to visualize this and you begin to really become honest about your answers your materials will take on a completely different perspective. Many times, you will begin to see just why prospects and customers do not react to your advertising, your marketing materials, or your sales presentation. You *must* be able to answer these two questions. If you can't, *you pull the material and go back to the drawing board.*

Clarity is the key to a business's ability to survive, thrive and grow.

A Coach's Advice: Where Baseball Meets Business

I've come to believe, based upon conversations I've had with clients I've worked with from around the world that our success in business and life is totally based on how hard we make it. And, believe me, we are our own worst enemies. In most cases the basics are ignored in favor of the latest new and, usually complex, fad or strategy, theory or latest bestseller unveiling the latest and greatest secrets to success.

But sometimes, most of the time in fact, if we just slow down we come face to face with the fact that success may be in the simplicity of the solution. Simple is not always easy. Simple is not always cool or flashy. But, SIMPLE works!

NIKE has built a worldwide brand on the simplest, yet most powerful positioning statement maybe ever devised with their "Just Do It" mantra. That simple three-word statement speaks volumes. Plan all you want, strategize until you're giddy, but to get anything done you will need to Just Do It at some point. Brilliant!

Coach Bob Brenly, the former coach of the Arizona Diamondback baseball club had an inspiring philosophy when it came to success. His tenure began in 2001, following a coach who was very clinical and ran the club with reams of rules and expectations. When Brenly arrived, players asked him about his rules. He is reported to have said that he only had three rules: 1) be on time, 2) play hard, 3) get the job done. That's all the coach asked. By the way, the Diamondbacks won the World Series in 2001.

Those same three rules are just as powerful when applied to building a success strategy for your business.

1. **Be on time:** You must show up for work. You, must be ready, be positive, be focused and prepared to concentrate! You must manage what time you have, doing only the most important, highest consequence tasks, to get you where you want to go!

2. **Play hard:** In today's marketplace you can have great strategies, plans, and intentions, but if you aren't willing to work really, really, really hard, then you are doomed. You'll make mistakes, and it won't be easy, but simply by working hard you'll be ahead of 90% of your competitors.

3. **Get the job done:** Be determined; Be disciplined to do whatever it takes to accomplish the job. Whatever . . . it

. . . takes!

Continuous learning and personal growth are key. But sometimes we need to take all our acquired knowledge and collectively boil it down to the simplest of applications. There's no real secret and there is no amazing "silver bullet." The true discipline really comes in the harshness of absolute simplicity. Every successful businessperson, at one time or another, has had to face this fact.

Share, Collaborate and Thrive

A client of mine recently spoke these words out of frustration and anger and with blinders on. And I quote, "Our internal collaboration sucks; we have none and I don't get it!" He was trying to point blame at everyone and everything, except the real issue: the business culture he created. His company is a focused and driven organization, but all the company's problems revolve around the fact that only one person is driving the car. My client, the boss and owner, runs his business using the antiquated "mushroom strategy", meaning that he believes in keeping all his employees and managers in the dark and covered in, shall we say, garbage. No discussion of strategy, no conversation with his teams, no open discussions and, you guessed it, no collaboration. Yet his frustration is focused on why no one works together or understands what they should be doing. As my grandson would say, "Dude, wake up and smell the . . ." Well you know what.

Successful businesses are those in which everyone talks and collaborates with each other—each department and every manager and leader from the top down. The goal, simply, is to communicate better and collaborate more. However, in a world defined by the power and use of information, some stagger around in an environment where communication and collaboration succumb to short-sighted fear of openness and sharing.

Collaboration at work is the ability to be open to new ideas, to be willing to share and have discussions without preconceived agendas. The goal of any business owner should be to nurture a spirit of innovation through a collaborative work environment. When this situation exists, the best ideas are shared, agreed upon, and eventually implemented. In scenarios like this, the business thrives, and the employees feel engaged—which creates a win for all parties.

Most start-ups that succeed in year one will have a rich story of collaboration. Start-ups that survive have created cohesive, open, and innovative work environments with everyone sharing the vision of what a successful future looks like. And, if a business has investors, active and open collaboration is the best way to keep them content.

What kind of team do you have in place? Do you have a shared vision? As a business leader, you need to be someone open to new ideas. One who is transparent and involves everyone in the company. Today, any business that needs to succeed must be entrepreneurial in its thinking and should constantly work to tear apart the old business mentality of, "that's the way we've always done it!" This kind of thinking will kill creativity and breed suspicion. Those create a bad work culture.

Collaboration means communicating well at work. If you cannot keep staff informed, they will wonder why they are there in the first place. Everyone from the receptionist to the field staff should have a clear vision and a passion for the company's growth. That's why a lot of employee-owned companies perform well. They believe in a shared responsibility to help one another, collaborate, and achieve success.

Businesses will not be productive if they do not collaborate. Collaboration brings in clarity and it helps leaders change and adapt well.

Do Your Homework and Beat the Odds! It's the statistic no one wants to pay attention to. It's that extra-long hair coming out of your nose that everyone sees but everyone wants to ignore. *Bloomberg* reports that eight out of ten entrepreneurial businesses will fail within their first eighteen months of existence. Research also says that thirty percent of all start-ups will continually lose money and that only nine percent even have a chance of surviving ten years.

Ask yourself honestly, do you still want to be an entrepreneur and start a new business? If the desire to build and own your own business still burns within you, here are a few ideas that might help you beat the odds.

1. **Research before you jump.** Before you take the plunge and start pumping all your (or someone else's) money into your project, research the industry you're moving into. I'm not talking about researching your business idea initially. I'm talking about looking into the specific industry category your business fits into. Understand what's happening within the industry and what the opportunities, roadblocks and warning signs might be. Smallbiztrends.com says the three highest-risk business categories are:

    a. Independent restaurants: sixty-percent failure rates. Owners are often skilled at their craft but not at business.

b. Retail stores: eighty-percent failure rate of retail clothing stores are largely due to poor management, fierce competition, and poor marketing.

c. Direct sales businesses: No matter the pitch, only twenty percent of retail products are purchased through direct sales reps and ninety-nine percent of direct sales reps suffer significant financial losses.

2. **Never decide for your potential customer what they will and what they won't like.** You can never be so enamored with an idea, or so convinced that you can make it work, that you don't ask the market what it wants. Being in the mindset that you know what your potential customers want and that they will buy what you have is a dangerous mindset indeed. One simple exercise I learned early on has, without fail, allowed my startups to roll out stronger and be profitable faster. We always created or acquired a list of every potential customer we could find. Then I would, with the help of whoever I could get, called every manager or owner on the list. Our telephone script was based on the idea that we were a new company about to enter their industry. We were not calling to sell them anything, but we were doing a simple two-question survey. We would then ask them (our future prospect) "What do you love about the vendors you work with?" and "What do you hate about the vendors you work with?" We would then let them talk and they would succinctly tell us what we should do and shouldn't do to get in their door and eventually sell to them. Our marketing plan and our business plans

were always adjusted to the requirements of the market.

3. **Being a good technician does not make you a good businessperson.** Just because your business idea is based on something you know how to do and are good at, does not mean that enthusiasm will make you a great businessperson. The two skills are separate. So always identify your strengths and weakness early and be honest with yourself. If you know you're not good with paperwork or numbers, hire an accountant. If you know you're not a great leader of people, hire a manager. If you're not a good salesperson, hire one. Unbalanced experience or a lack of managerial experience usually leads to a level of incompetence that could drive your business into the gutter.

4. **Create an absolutely clear and powerful value proposition.** You must know what your Unique Value Proposition is without a doubt. What truly sets you apart from your competition? What is it that you or your product does that you can do faster, cheaper, stronger, with additional quality, and do more profitably? How can you save the customer time or money or improve the quality of their life? Once you have these things identified, apply the "acid test" questions. State your value propositions one by one and ask yourself "SO WHAT?", "WHAT'S IN IT FOR ME?" Believe me, your prospects will be asking these same questions. If you can't answer these questions, start over!

5. **Write a comprehensive business plan.** No matter how small your start-up is, I always strongly recommend that you write a business plan. Even if nobody sees it

but you, write it. The Business Plan process forces you to ask yourself hard questions about the viability of your idea; how you plan to sell and market your product or service; who and who your buyers might be. You might also discover that you need to tweak or outright change your initial idea. Don't argue on this one. Just do it. It will be worth your time! By the way, if you ever want to raise money for your business, your answers will be required.

There are plenty of other things that you can do to avoid the pitfalls of an entrepreneurial start-up, but these five will get you started.

Take Action and Find Opportunity!

Okay, I know everybody has advice on business. Everyone must get a word in on the economy. But being the optimist that I am, I wanted to find out what top businesspeople are saying and, more importantly, *doing* to ensure they do not just survive but they *thrive* in this challenging economy. Realistically, when you look closely, you'll see there are businesses in almost every market sector that are having record years and selling plenty of products and services.

When you start to dig for information and do a little research, you'll find there are elemental business practices that every thriving business today is doing. The great news is, YOU CAN THRIVE TOO! This is not rocket science, its business. It's time to stop blaming the economy. It's time to do something about it!

1. **Don't panic yourself out of business.** In other words, don't drink the Kool-Aid.

You must understand WHAT IS versus WHAT IF. Accept the WHAT IS and base your strategy on that. What is your reality? I asked a struggling customer the other day just how the economy has affected him, and he said, "Oh, it hasn't, but it could!" Remember, optimism leads to action, and passivity leads to paralysis.

2. **There's opportunity everywhere.** Understand that ninety percent of businesses have given up or are in hiding, scared of the *what if*. What if this would happen? What if that would happen? What if the economy tanks? What if we have more taxes? What if a piece of the space station fell off, plummeted to earth, and crashed on top of my car? What if? Stop it! It's time to go on the offensive. Forget about finding new business, go steal market share, steal customers from your competitors while they're on the sidelines worrying about all the things they cannot control.

3. **Understand the customer's needs from the customer's point of view.** The day of providing products and services in the way you think is best for your customers, is over. There are too many options out there for customers. Because of that, there's even less brand loyalty. So, you had better slow down and find ways to find out what your prospects and customers want, from *their* point of view . . . then you had better deliver it. Do a survey; read industry reports; understand consumer buying habits, do something.

4. **Run your business like a "bootstrap" start-up.** No matter how long you've been around, no matter how big you are, and no matter how successful you've been, you

absolutely need to step back and look at your company as if it was brand new. Protect your cash. Watch your spending. Focus solely on sales. Take extra great care of your customers. Take even better care of your employees. Trim fat and focus on what's important.

5. **Set goals.** Most experts say that in our society, seventy percent of us do not set goals. Twenty-eight percent say they set goals and less than two percent of us actually have written goals. Many go on to say that the two percent with written goals control ninety-eight percent of today's income. Set personal goals and set business goals and write them down. Brian Tracy says, "Success is goals . . . all else is commentary!"

6. **Don't waste a penny of your marketing budget.** This is the biggest issue that I deal with daily. Know if your marketing is or isn't working. If you don't know, shame on you. You need to find out right now. If you know it isn't working, STOP it today. Don't continue spending and utilizing elements of your marketing just because "that's the way we've always done it!" Today's consumer, *your* consumer, has dramatically changed, and you need to understand where they're at and how to reach them. Don't spend another penny until you figure that out.

7. **Solve problems and make decisions.** "The things that matter most should never be at the mercy of the things that matter least." Johann Wolfgang von Goethe, German writer and statesman, spoke those words in 1780. And they could not be truer today when it comes to prioritizing and managing your time. Don't sit on problems and hope they go away. In today's market

indecision will cost you sales and customers. The world will not wait for you to figure out what to do. Act now and continue moving forward.

8. **Manage your time.** American success guru, Brian Tracy said, "There's never enough time to do everything, but there's always enough time to do the right thing." Your only focus should be on how to make more sales, acquire customers, and then retain the customers you have. Anything else is a waste of your valuable time. Always stop and ask yourself, "Is this the number one thing/ task that I should be doing RIGHT NOW to move my business forward?"

9. **Remember that someone is always watching.** Your attitude reflects on you all the time. You cannot afford to have a bad or down attitude. Your employees are watching, and they will reflect your approach to business and life at work. Your bankers, partners, suppliers, and distributors are all watching to see how you react. You may not see them watching, but they are. Research done by the Carnegie Institute says that a full eighty-five percent of all success is based on attitude! Not skill, not knowledge, but attitude. Sam Walton of Walmart fame was once asked how the terrible recession that the United States was in, had affected Walmart. Mr. Walton was said to have said, "It hasn't affected us at all." The surprised mob of reporters, as one, asked how that could be. Sam Walton then said, "Simple. We chose not to participate."

So, what is the attitude you're carrying around? Is it positive, confident, and hopeful? Or, is it stressed, angry and unsure? Be aware of what people see in you. Your personal and professional career may be at stake.

10. **Hang with winners.** Surround yourself with like-minded businesspeople. If your normal crowd is always moaning, groaning, and complaining, as hard as it might be, find new friends and associates. Attitude rubs off, either way. Stay positive and feed on the possibility-thinking people who "get it."

11. **Never, Never, Never Give Up.** Keep pushing. Keep trying and always believe in yourself. Enough said.

My Annual Declaration of TOTAL Business Independence

Every year, on the 4th of July, I like to publish the annual version of My Declaration of TOTAL Business Independence. I like to update and, in a sense, re-imagine my declaration each year because, if you haven't noticed, the pace of progress and what it takes to be personally and professionally successful gets more demanding every year.

So how has your year gone so far? Can you answer? Do you even know? You should know exactly how your year has gone—and the key word here is *exactly*. Based on the clarity of your answer, you will soon know which things you are doing or not doing to achieve the clarity you need to thrive.

- You are, or aren't, using written goals to measure your success or lack thereof.

- You are, or aren't, tracking everything from personal productivity to sales success.

- You are, or you aren't, prioritizing your daily tasks and only doing the most important things to drive you towards your professional and personal goals.

- You are, or you aren't, managing by objective. You either do or do not know what your sales are against your goals for the week, month, quarter, year, and previous year.

- You are, or you are not, dealing in REALITY.

If you follow my success philosophy, you know your success or lack of success is largely based on your perception of reality. For me, when my personal Independence Day comes around, the year is half over, but it's also a time of opportunity, a time to adjust, a time for new and improved beginnings. We should only look at the past six months to analyze what we are doing well and where improvement is needed. Then, with that information, we can make valuable course corrections.

Everything we do, and should do, is based on the singular goal of becoming an independent and successful entrepreneur, manager, executive, and/or business owner. The only way to achieve this goal is to constantly be in search of ways to get better, to analyze the past to make the future great. Sometimes this is achieved simply by committing to a level of excellence in the basic foundational and proven factors of success. You don't need to wait until the 4th of July to assess, get serious, knuckle down and get the job done. If you haven't done that already, do so now. Now may also be a good time to review or even (dare I say) create your goals.

It's time to confidently make concrete and rock-solid commitments to certain disciplines and thoughts that have proven through time to be the foundation of successful and profitable sales, marketing, and business practices.

So, to that end, I offer up my updated Annual Declaration of Business Independence.

My Annual Declaration of Business Independence

1. I will not listen to the naysayers, negative friends and business acquaintances, the networks, the TV news, the business magazines and talking heads. I understand that I will create my own future and completely control my own environment as what I believe it is. I can and will make my business better and I will always win!

2. I will set goals and objectives and write them down to achieve my dream. (A dream pushes you to do something out of the ordinary and your goals help you make your dream a reality.)

3. I will clearly understand my "why" and will shift my marketing away from "selling" to "helping." (No one likes to be sold, but everyone likes to get help.)

4. I will not waste money on marketing, and I understand that all my marketing has been wasted when I didn't know whether it was working or not. I must track everything.

5. I will not dedicate my budgets to marketing fads. I will analyze and understand every tool available and know if my target customer and market can be reached with these methods.

6. I will become a master listener. I will clearly understand my prospects' and clients' needs from their point of view

7. I will work to build trust through everything that I do and say. Trust is the basis for strong relationships and

sales.

8. I will replace sales lingo in my marketing with natural and conversational language. It's much easier to engage a prospect with a conversation than with a prepared speech that tells them what I think they want to know.

9. I will measure the effectiveness of every aspect of my marketing and sales process and continually test alternatives to improve my conversion rates and my sales. No matter how good my marketing is, I can always improve it.

10. I will discover alternative ways to close the sale that aren't pushy or uncomfortable. I will listen more, ask more questions, and then respond to the customer's needs.

11. I will avoid wasting time and money trying to reinvent the wheel and will ask for help from experts and trusted advisors when I find myself struggling.

12. I will become a time management maniac. I vow to never waste my time. I will delegate all the tasks someone else could do. (I can't grow my business if I'm spending my time sorting email or running to the post office.)

13. I will create a daily plan for how I can maximize the use of my time and I will follow it to maximize sales. Without a plan, I'll never get around to developing that new product, service or implementing my marketing strategy.

So, I encourage you to look at the coming months with an eye to the future instead of issues from the past. Focus and make this the best year of your life!

Change: Relax and Accept It

We often hear that change is the only constant in life, and it's true. But we also hear that lots of businesses fail because they cannot deal with change. That is also true, but why?

As a business coach, I often meet leaders who say they cannot deal with change. They complain that because of the pace of change in the world, their productivity is low, employee morale has fallen, and they cannot visualize what's coming at them. Yes, there are rapid changes in technology and the way we do business, but we must face change with boldness, confidence, and an entrepreneurial spirit. Basically, any businessperson must be willing to accept change.

My simple advice is that all business leaders must develop a mindset for change. A mindset for change is simple—it gives you a roadmap to follow the basic business principles of obtaining clarity, managing time efficiently, and always staying focused on your real, worthy objectives.

We must do whatever it takes to always be prepared for change. What worked yesterday more than likely will not work tomorrow. What you have done the same way for years will soon not exist. Innovation and change are now constant. So, the new mindset paradigm is to forget the old, conservative ways of holding on to "the way it's always been done." For example, how many people or businesses still use the fax machine? Aren't we seeing the slow demise of the personal computer? When they were first launched, how did we react to that change?

An old and trusted mentor has always said, "If you continue to conduct business the way you've always conducted business, you most assuredly will soon be out of business." I believe he is right on!

So, the mantra is to be willing to change and, just as importantly, focus yourself to see the need for change. Automaker and entrepreneur, Henry Ford, was quoted as saying, "If I had asked people what they want, they would have said a faster horse."

Take the story of Blockbuster. For decades, Blockbuster was a required stop on a Friday evening: rent a couple of movies, eat popcorn, and relax. However, with the advent of Netflix, all of that changed. Change killed a product, a culture, and a lifestyle. Blockbuster's leaders knew change was coming but didn't do anything about it.

During times of rapid change, we should focus on pursuing the great opportunities that change brings in its fold. We should not lose sight that our end goal in business is to run a business successfully, and efficiently. The best way is to handle change is in increments, taking the time to understand what it entails. For instance, if one of your new divisions requires a technology that can increase efficiency and bring in greater profits, make sure you act fast before your competitors get their hands on it. Change requires you to be nimble, agile, and ready to adapt to a fast-changing world.

One great detriment that I have seen among business leaders facing change is their fear to deal with change itself. They fear reduced income, loss of markets and total chaos. But remember, if you have the mindset for change, you can easily overcome obstacles. Smart businesses will constantly inform their employees of impending change, educate and train them fast on handling change and, above all else, do everything they can to improve their morale and productivity. During times of change, it is critical to gain employee confidence by informing them of what's happening. And remember to inform everyone, not just your inner circle. This is vitally important because honest feedback from your employees regarding change will help you make the kind of rapid adjustments essential for tackling the needs of the market. Make sure your employees are thoroughly trained to deal with new technologies and new thought processes in producing and selling your products. Do not dump stuff on them and hope that they understand what you want them to say or do.

During times of change, great innovation occurs. Smart leaders experiment and fail. It's okay to fail during times of change, but with the right mindset, a mindset of accepting and even welcoming change, you can jump back fast and focus on the next big thing coming at you. Today, change is like chasing a storm. When you think it has gone away, it comes roaring back at you. When it comes back, only your mindset can save you.

So, do you have the mindset for change? If not, do you need help creating a mindset for change and accelerating your business and personal life? Do all you can to acquire and keep an openness to the necessity of change in both your personal and professional life. If you don't, nothing will change!

Clarity Through Metrics

If I had a nickel for every time I've heard the word *metrics* being tossed around, I would be rich. Okay, I see I'm on my simplicity kick again but, depending who you listen to, defining metrics can be akin to the scientific formula for the origins of the universe. Keep it simple my business friends. Metrics can be several things, including goals, expectations, and simply defining the difference between an average job, a good job and a great job. A metric helps us define accountability in what we do. Once we know what accountability is, we can define consequences (good and bad) and reward or reprimand someone on the metrics that are the basis of performance.

Metrics are the pathway for us to find out what "good" looks like in our businesses. Let's take this example of three types of people, the ones living in poverty, the ones in the middle class, and those who are very rich. Each one is defined by a certain set of metrics that can include what our government says they are. But each group also has its own set of metrics that clearly define their personal metrics for classification. One group may go to bed hungry every night, the other argues what kind of caviar they will have for dinner.

As an entrepreneur or a manager of a startup business, you can't ask or expect people to excel unless they clearly understand how their success will be measured. Let me give you a story of an interaction I had with a client. For several years his sales staff was on a fixed salary. They did not have any performance goals except to show up for work and sell something. When they didn't sell something, he would yell at them! I began to talk with him about the logical benefits of a commission program that was specifically pegged to meeting and exceeding goals. This led to a period of hair pulling and gnashing of teeth. His attitude was that this action would be intrusive and demoralizing to his sales staff. How dare the business owner ask the sales staff to be held accountable for specific sales numbers. How dare him!

Ironically, one of the biggest curmudgeons of the group figured out the value of rewards based on metrics and before long this guy was knocking down some considerable NEW income. Long story short, it wasn't then long before everybody was on the bandwagon and the resulting sales and business growth was nothing short of phenomenal.

A metric can be anything really. A metric can be a specific number, a specific goal, or a specific expectation. But it must be specific, and it must be written.

Metrics are ultimately of great consequence in both our business lives and in our personal lives. In my case, I have made it a discipline to establish my business/personal metrics for the next day, and review the full week, every night before going to bed. Part of that "priority and time management plan" is to focus on establishing five "prospect" meetings a week. When I achieve my goal, I have twenty meetings every month, making me one of the highest performing business coaches in my arena of expertise. I focus on my challenges and accomplish them.

One of the great and universal keys to success is disciplining yourself to always strive for clarity about specifically what it is that success looks like for each task. Clarifying the gray and fuzzy edges and establishing absolute purity in your vision of any task or goal is the secret. The difference between average and the great today is in the understanding of that one principle. Always look for clarity and eliminate any randomness from your personal or business life. If you don't, expect a lifetime of wasted time and frustration. Yes, it could be that bad!

So, happy tomorrow! Don't be afraid of clarity through metrics. You can start today, it's never too late!

Every Business Needs a CEO

I was recently asked by a local business network organization to sit on a panel for a discussion about small business growth issues. On the panel were a couple of small business owners, an entrepreneur, a sole-proprietor business owner, and the owner of a large business. I filled the position of the resident business coach and business-growth advisor.

The discussion turned to the topic of the importance of titles in a business. I've never cared much for titles, but I do understand their significance as a business strategy. However, I have a new attitude toward titles, and I explained it to this audience. You see, I had just finished a great book called, *The Energy Bus* by Jon Gordon. Mr. Gordon has written several bestselling books about personal energy and the effect that enhanced energy can bring to reduce your stress and transform your life and business.

What I shared at that event was that I believe every business should have a CEO. That's right, a CEO, but not the CEO of traditional definition. In *The Energy Bus*, Jon Gordon defines a CEO as the Chief Energy Officer. As the CEO or Chief Energy Officer, you become the driving force of your business. The one person who believes you WILL be successful, that nothing can stand in your way; not competition, not a bad economy, not bad attitudes. The Chief Energy Officer believes nothing can or is standing in the way of moving forward with a positive and winning attitude, every hour, every day, every week of every month. With that attitude, instead of just surviving, your business will be transformed and will thrive! The Chief Energy Officer is a title I can support and understand—and believe is necessary. At some point, the title can be and should be transferred to a manager or even a group of employees, but in today's market and the business world, this type of CEO is a necessity. It's all about creating a positive perceived value, one that begins with *you,* the business owner. It is a value that will be seen by employees and anyone else who is or will be important to the growth of your business.

Hey, What Went *Right Here?*

I'm always amazed at how much time is spent in business pointing fingers, looking for blame, finding fault, and holding endless meetings about what went wrong, who screwed up and why. Countless upon countless hours, weeks and months are wasted and lost dealing with the negative intentions of what went wrong.

Kathryn Shulz is known as the World's Leading Wrongologist. She studies just how faulty the standard business practice of "looking for wrong" is. She says, "We have the power to understand what we did right and what we did wrong and make change. We can say that we made a mistake and change and learn from it!" The key word here is LEARN. However, most of the time LEARN is not the focus, and, BLAME is.

In my business coaching practice, I demand my clients get out of the negative habits of wasting time, thus wasting money, when they go on regular witch hunts when something goes wrong. The old-school business approach to problems, when something goes wrong is to say, "Let form a committee to discover who screwed up." So, after months of stupid meetings and an incredible amount of unprofitable man hours, someone is fingered and singled out and humiliated. Meanwhile, in more forward-thinking times nimble companies, both large and small, take a different approach. Their approach is one of learning from the mistake or problem and then moving on.

Here are my four essential rules. This is our new mantra and standard for dealing with all issues:

1. What do we distinctly know about what happened?

2. What did we learn?

3. What are we going to change so this won't happen again?

4. This is all the time we're going to spend on that issue. Rearview mirror thinking is DONE, and we move forward with new knowledge.

Here's a powerful and cool alternative to a "what went wrong" session. From this point forward, create a "right way" notebook. Instead of focusing on the negative, use the same time that in the past you've allocated to finding blame, to analyzing what you, your staff and your company is doing *right*!

Many times, we find that companies are spending so much time protecting themselves from what could go wrong that they neglect what is going right. We can reverse that trend. I urge business owners to spend focused time on all systems and processes and become acutely aware of what *is* working. Then understand, precisely, why the approach or strategy is working. Document it completely and then use your time to work on ways to ensure continuous improvement.

Do this and you will see a major shift from negative to

positive taking place in your business and you'll begin to build more and more successful processes and strategies that tend to build on each other. This inevitably begins to drive future success and higher profits—and that, my dear friend, is always good!

How to Be a Better Manager

Sometimes, to be better at what we do, we just need a reminder. In those rare moments when we have sat quietly trying to figure things out, we sometimes just need that little tap on the shoulder, that slight thump on the forehead, or maybe a hearty kick in the butt to be made aware that there is a learning opportunity right here, right now. A little voice that says, "Hey, remember this and things will be easier." I try to remind clients that success in business, leadership, and management doesn't always come from an MBA or a book. Most of the time the best solutions come from others who have already been down this path and learned something from the journey. A friend of mine used to call that, OPE (Other Peoples Experiences). That's the key.

So, friends here you go, fourteen reminders based totally on OPE, on ways to be a better manager.

1. **Understand your responsibilities**. Know your part in the company and how to do your job so well that goals, objectives, and client demands aren't just met, they're exceeded. Before you can expect your employees to give you 100% demonstrate that you will give 110%.

2. **Be a great listener.** A great manager knows how to listen to his employees as well as superiors. Take the time to listen. Show them their opinion and input are valuable to

you and the company.

3. **Practice and teach priority management.** Know how much time needs to be allotted to reaching your highest priority goals and objectives. Be realistic when making promises. Remember the 80/20 rule. Eighty percent of your results will come from twenty percent of your activities.

4. **Communicate, communicate, communicate.** As head of the team, it's your job to know how everyone on the team is doing. Make sure the team knows they can come to you with questions or concerns. If they feel comfortable coming to you, then you'll form a solid working relationship based on trust.

5. **Show appreciation.** Don't just talk to your team when problems arise. Hand out praise and encouragement, versus spending your time looking for them to be doing something wrong. Be different. Be unique. Spend your time looking for those things they are doing right. Showing appreciation will only motivate them to exceed their current level of performance.

6. **Be considerate and fair.** When problems and conflicts arise, don't show favoritism. Always resolve conflicts the same way every time regardless of who is involved.

7. **Look like a manager.** Wear an appropriate wardrobe, be clean and orderly. Set the standard for all reporting to you.

8. **Be sure your staff has access to all the information needed to do their job.** This should always include a detailed description of what "good" looks like for that job.

9. **Share information.** Be sure your people KNOW how their

work fits into the big picture, including company goals and the progress of the organization.

10. **Avoid micromanaging.** Too much direction, too many reporting requirements, too many meetings stifle creativity, ruin time management, and waste time the employee could use productively.

11. **Encourage your people to grow and expand their capabilities.** Don't be afraid to nurture your own replacement.

12. **Make your expectations clear.** Never be vague. Be sure your people understand that they are responsible for the tasks you assign.

13. **Encourage employees to have initiative.** If you want robots, buy robots. But if you want real people with ideas and emotions and initiative, then encourage them to create and improvise and discuss their ideas and thoughts.

14. **Find out what your people like to do most,** then focus them on tasks that fit their skills.

Take the time to think about the little simple things you can do to be a better manager. I guarantee that it will turn into profits for your entire organization.

I Want It Now!

I am not ashamed to say I am the guy in the technology section of any store who is standing there with big eyes, my jaw dropped, uttering strange giggling sounds, and randomly stricken by wild outbursts of "no way" and "wow."

I am continually astonished at the never-ending display of new and evolving technology. My career has allowed me to, many times, be on the cutting edge of new technology and I remain starstruck. Maybe it's my age, maybe I'm still a kid inside . . . but not a kid of today. And, my friends, the youth of today are changing everything. Here's why.

According to many of the world-class technologists I am privileged to know, we are not even scratching the surface of what is possible. In fact, many will say that everything we now know and understand will be obsolete in less than two years.

Obsolete!

Obsolete?

Obsolete!!!

With the consistent and aggressive growth of technology that affects all areas of our life and world, something interesting is happening. A fundamental shift in how today's consumer thinks is changing everything. If you're a businessperson and you don't adjust to this shift it could be the end of your business.

In my thriving business workshops, the first rule we discuss is "If you continue to do business the way you've always done business . . . you WILL be out of business!" The backbone of this rule is based upon the way in which today's prime consumers are thinking, which dictates how they buy. Where most anyone over forty-something remembers a time not long ago where they were doing business without cell phones and computers, today's prime marketing age groups do not know a time without cell phones and computers. Look at the situation as a generational thing. I'm a baby boomer and have been using computers for only part of my life. My son is forty and he has been using computers since he was about eleven. His son is sixteen and has been online since he was three. The possibilities of modern technology are all they know. My grandson and his father have come to crave and *expect* companies to deliver goods and services in certain ways.

So, here's the business challenge: While I'm still in awe by emerging technology, this and future generations of consumers simply expect technology and its advancement. If you have a business and you are not available to your consumers in ways they expect you to be, they WILL go somewhere else to find a business that caters to their technology needs. And keep in mind when I say "technology" I mean things as simple as having a website. As unlikely as it seems, I work with many struggling businesses who still do not have a website!

There simply are too many options for consumers to shop somewhere else for your product or service. There is little to no loyalty. Their mantra is "How can I get the product, service or information I want when I want it, how I want it, and at the price I want it?"

Like it or not, that is what business today is all about— satisfying the customer's needs—truly, now more than ever, *from the customer's point of view.* If you are still only making your business available to your prime consumers through old technology, you should find a good business broker. You have no choice. Your present and future customers simply expect it, and, if you can't deliver you will be replaced about as fast as it takes to say GOOGLE.

If You Can Make It Better ... Do So

My life as a Master Business Coach is extremely gratifying. I love to see my clients break out of survival mode and experience life by thriving and growing daily. I love my job, most of the time. But in the last couple of weeks I've had to deal with some people who are extremely closed and inflexible, no matter how painful this approach is to them. They are stubborn, bullheaded, close-minded, scared of failure, and sometimes scared of success. Even though I am always frustrated with these people, I still will work with them because I believe in them, and their passion for what they're doing even if it is unfocused. The situation reminds me like that annual childhood holiday experience of having to kiss that big old, blue-haired aunt who wore too much perfume and had a long hair sprouting from her chin. You don't want to do it, but you must.

To be honest, working with clients like this just drives me nuts. Why do around ninety percent of all new businesses fail? I'm beginning to believe the cause is simply a lack of willingness to change, adapt, improvise, and adjust to the ever-so-rapidly-changing needs of consumers. I do a workshop seminar entitled: Don't Just Survive but Thrive in Any Economy! We discuss seven primary factors to consider when planning for your ongoing business.

You must be agile and open to change. You must have a mentality that accepts change. With rapidly advancing technology that affects every part of our life, you must believe that anything *is* possible. That one unknown person with a great idea on how to do something, anything, better can and does change the world. But you must believe it. A friend of mine recently sent me an email on this subject. Here are a few examples that he points out about how an idea about how something could be done better has changed our world:

- Smart phones have virtually eliminated the point-and-shoot camera market

- Netflix & Redbox and iTunes have eliminated the

movie rental store

- Amazon has led to the demise of the brick-and-mortar bookstore

- Wikipedia destroyed the hard copy edition of *Encyclopedia Britannica*

- And ironically, Facebook has all but crushed the need for high school reunions

We must know if our strategies to build your business (if you have any strategies in the first place) are working. Build on them if they are, cut your losses as quickly as possible if they aren't. But never, and I mean never, get locked into a process that you are not willing to change, adjust or drop. The fact is, running and growing a business is hard work and the sure way to fail is to not be willing to admit that an idea, process, or strategy is not working. That's just ego talking and a sure, quick, and painful end to your business. Oh, you can always blame an advisor or blame the economy or higher prices or lower demand, but today that just doesn't fly. Consumers now have too many options and choices and the days of being the only option are gone. The fact is, somewhere there is some kid in his dad's garage tinkering with an idea that will change the world and could instantly make your product or business obsolete.

The only protection you might have is continually looking for ways to change your world through your own innovation and continuous improvement.

Invest in Your Business
by Investing in Your Employees

Surprise! It turns out many unhappy, unsatisfied, or disgruntled employees today don't always want a raise in pay.

Holy cow! What did I just say?

The research is interesting and may surprise you if you're an employer of any size. A recent Harvard Business Review report shows that employee satisfaction with their job and employee retention revolve around much more than just a raise in pay. The truth about what employees are looking for is simple.

Here's what employees want. They will, of course, be appreciative of a pay raise to acknowledge a job well done. However, they would really like other considerations, sometimes, equally as much or more. They want help to get better at their job. They want to know you care about them getting better at their job. The HBR reports show that *employer-provided training* has the same effect on job satisfaction as a 17.7% net wage increase. This is according to a study of nearly 5,000 workers. Other studies show that when these reports show low productivity gains from training, they are significantly overlooking the subjective benefits of on-the-job learning.

This information is an important warning for all business owners and executives in our current business climate. Business development experts have been screaming for years that for businesspeople to grow their businesses and protect their investment they must invest in the training and personal and professional growth of their staffs. In my business coaching practice, I work with many business owners whose idea of investing in their business revolves primarily around marketing. We also know that research repeatedly shows that the most successful and highest earning businesspeople, executives, and entrepreneurs are the ones who have a consistent and lifelong personal education program.

Implementing an employee training program for your business isn't that hard and does not need to be expensive to start. It might begin by simply bringing a few selections from your personal business book library for employees to share and read. The same goes for providing audio CDs for employees to check out and listen to. These powerful programs are readily available and economical at the same time. There are some incredible audio programs available from some of the greats in the business world that could greatly impact your staff. There is incredible material available on topics of goal setting, time management, business basics, leadership and sales.

If you want to ramp it up, do some investigation and then bring in a professional to do a workshop or clinic on specific subjects. You might want to hire a business coach to work with your team or even work with you personally. Whatever you do, it will pay off in multiples. You just need to commit to doing it! It doesn't work to just think about it.

Good intentions will only make you feel better while your business fails.

The bottom line is that employee retention is essential to building a great business. Look at it this way, the longer a good employee is with you the more you have invested in them anyway, so make a commitment to help them to their next level, because when you do that your business grows right along with them. And remember to give them a pat on the back while you're at it! It will pay dividends.

It's YOU Who Counts

Have you ever noticed how a certain business location can seem to be cursed? It's the place where businesses go to die, and then an owner comes along that thrives in the same location. What was the difference between all the others that did not survive and the one that thrived?

It's usually the owner's attitude towards success.

Now don't get me wrong, I'm sure everyone who starts a business wants to be successful, but are they prepared for success?

When I say you must be prepared for success, it is not a trick statement. It is that simple. If you've ever had a house built, you know you don't just go to a builder and say, "Build me a house, I want to move in next week!" That won't happen without some thought and planning, and the same thought and planning must go into starting a business.

Prepare for success by planning and planning some more. The unbreakable rule when you start a business (and I've started fourteen of them) is NO SURPRISES! Surprises will shut you down.

Here are a few of the things you can do to be prepared for successfully starting a business:

1. **Be positive** no matter what your challenges are. How your attitude goes, so goes everyone around you including employees and customers and sales and profitability.

2. **Write a business plan** even if no one else but you will see it. Take the time to write one and ask yourself all the questions required.

3. **Do three to five financial models.** Running the numbers means you'll need to do some research on things like:
   - Various rent scenarios
   - Best vendor pricing on merchandise or related services
   - Various advertising and marketing costs
   - Insurance and utilities
   - Payroll projections
   - And if the numbers don't work, back off the project no matter how badly you want it.

4. **Capitalization.** Be sure you have enough money to survive and stick to managing the money you do have.

5. **Matching Skills.** Clearly know if your business idea is complementary to your talents.

6. **Workable time frames.** Always have a reasonable time window on getting the business up and running. Have you set, or are you up against, unreasonable deadlines?

7. **Nerve.** And finally, for this short list, always be sure your head is in the right place to start, run and endure the rigors of business ownership.

"Please Take Me with You!"
The Power of Employee Engagement

A few weeks ago, a friend of mine had a great opportunity and accepted a new job. There was the traditional farewell party in which some co-workers gave him going-away cards. He shared with me one that was quite interesting. The card, from a now "former" colleague simply said, "Please take me with you!"

When we discuss employee engagement in a workplace, this is one of the worst testimonies ever. I believe everyone wants to work in a culture where they feel appreciated as an integral part of the team. Unfortunately, many workplaces are filled with employees with a hidden and powerful emotional agenda to get out as fast as they possibly can.

The workplace culture defines how we interact and commit to our jobs in a fast-changing environment. According to Neil Patel, in an article in *Quicksprout Newsletter*, Patel confidently says he will reject any candidate who has all the work skills but lacks the fit necessary for joining his company's work culture.

Zappos, too, is committed to the power of this concept. That's why they pay prospective employees to try out their workplace culture before they commit to a full-time position.

So, how can we create a culture where we can keep employees happy and productive? It all begins with hiring people who are smarter and more talented than you. Hire people who are thirsty for new knowledge and who have a craving to improve your business and be part of a dynamic team. They may not be the highest paid executives in your line of work but will be eager to work collaboratively and with a positive spirit.

"Look for the ones who crave success, who have that innate hunger to do bold things and constantly improve. Seek out employees who are good at developing and sustaining efficient processes," says Patel. I also recommend finding and hiring the candidates who have clarity and know where they want to go because they will help you succeed. So, "hire hungry and keep them happy!"

Employers should look beyond hiring smart to create a

work culture that enhances productivity. This can only come through employee retention and we all know the high costs of employee turnover.

In my opinion, high employee turnover occurs at institutions where upper management was not hired right the first time. If you had great leaders, your employees wouldn't have left so quickly.

However, businesses often make the common mistake of hiring senior leaders by looking at their previous stature, compensation history, and growth trajectory. Remember, there is a fundamental mistake here. Most often, you will miss the "entrepreneurial" types your business often needs to succeed.

So, the next time an employee leaves your business, do an objective assessment of what happened. And, if there is something wrong with your work culture, remember that change must start at the top.

Is your business facing workplace culture issues? Are people saying, "please take me with you" to every colleague that leaves? If so, you need to act fast and decisively to protect your businesses and your personal future.

Networking: Learn It, Like It or Lose

All right gang, it's time for a pop quiz. Can you tell me how many times you've networked with someone online or in person and exchanged ideas and thoughts regarding your business in the last week? If your answer is less than three, you're in trouble.

According to *Webster's Dictionary*, networking means "interchanging information or services among a group of persons or organizations." There is absolutely, positively, no time better than now to start building your networks to grow your business and personal contacts. You cannot live secluded with your own ideas in this fast-changing business environment that we live in. If you are, pull your head out of the sand and figure this "networking thing" out! Start off small and keep it simple, but networking is becoming a critical business skill.

In a world dominated by new modes of communication, we have no choice but to connect with others and gain new knowledge regarding running our businesses. Let me give you an example of the power of connectivity and how it can influence the way we work and build networks. Recently, a top GE executive told a business marketing conference in Phoenix Arizona how they sourced a new design for an aircraft part. GE, with 18,000 engineers on its rolls opened a design competition worldwide to find out who could provide a new, "outside the box" kind of design for this particular aircraft part. Despite its vast internal resources, the best design was sourced from an Indonesian college student. You need to build your networks NOW. Your competition is now global and is not limited by territory or skills. Smart businesspeople know how to find opportunity, build great networks, and disrupt old ways of thinking. Technology is the new equalizer.

Here are some key steps for building your network:

- Be clear of exactly which market you want to dominate. Identify peers in your industry who can connect you with influencers and seek their guidance.

- Don't network just to network. Be sure to understand who your target is and where they hang out. Always hang where the decision makers hang!

- Don't be shy. When you attend meetings, make it a point to introduce yourself to the speaker or the main personalities. Always give them your business card and connect with them in twenty-four hours or less.

- Use LinkedIn, definitely use LinkedIn! It's the Facebook for business these days. Do not hesitate to connect with folks and join groups linked to your industry. Try to post valid comments in group discussions and be an active player in connecting with your network.

- Try to do informational interviews with people in your industry. This will help you connect with other influential contacts who know the people you need to know.

- Networking meetings need not be expensive lunches or dinners. The easiest way is to invite like-minded folks for coffee.

- As you learn more through networking, remember to pass on your knowledge and contacts to others. Be authentic in your thoughts and ways of sharing knowledge.

- Good networking will help you get great references as you seek a job, a major contract, or look for your next promotion.

- Seek "sponsors", not mentors within and outside your organization. A great sponsor will be able to talk about you to others within and outside your network.

The key is being smart about your networking. The goal is not to go to an event and give, then get, 100 business cards. So what? I would bet that out of that 100 you received at a random event that only one person who attended was actually a decision maker. Be strategic and make your networking efforts a valuable use of your time. Network for profit. Anything else, and you're just going to a cocktail party.

Riding for the Brand

"If you hire people just because they can do a job, they'll work for your money. But if you hire people who believe what YOU believe, they'll work for you with blood, sweat and tears."

SIMON SINEK

I have a great deal of appreciation for those hardy souls that we know as "frontiersman" or "pioneers", particularly the ones who opened the American West. This is the stock that I am proud to say I descended from. My grandfather lived in a dugout on the side of a creek in south-central Kansas as a child. It took a lot of hard work, hard living conditions, incredible fortitude and spirit for him and people like him to endure what they had to endure to create the freedom the West represented. In my way of thinking, our pioneering forefathers were some of the first entrepreneurs. They had a dream and worked hard to achieve it. If you study this period there are many lessons that can be applied to current business conditions.

One of those lessons that I often refer to with coaching clients is a powerful lesson in team building and hiring. The issue is not necessarily one of getting people to work together, but one of building a team of strong employees, managers, and leadership that want to work with you and your business because they *believe in* you and your business. Case in point . . . during the days of huge cattle drives from Texas to shipping depots in Kansas, each ranch had its own form of recognition, known as their "brand." That brand was literally burned on the hide of each head of cattle to distinguish the animal as part of that herd. The cowboys tending the cattle drive would be known then to "ride for the brand." Rain or shine, through blizzards or unbearable heat, day in, day out, the cowboys would work for around $15 a month. The cowboys worked in incredible conditions for low pay, but they believed in the ranch owner and his brand. Sometimes they would even die for that brand.

In today's market, the brand is your business. So, the question is, "Who in your business, from the top-level executives to the guys in the yard, are working for a paycheck or riding for the brand?" This is an essential question for every manager or business owner to ask themselves on a consistent basis. You must routinely evaluate each staff member using this question as a base. Business today is tough, it's challenging, and as an owner or manager, you had better *know* that you have a cohesive team that's working together, one that "has your back", a team that is riding for the brand.

Another way to put this question is to ask yourself this: if your competition called and said they were coming over to have it out once and for all with a rumble in the street, could you stand tall, gather your confidence, march out to the parking lot and say, "All right team, who's with me" and there would be people lining up beside you? Put names to those you think would line up to support you. Or would *anyone* line up with you for the fight? You had better know the answer. In business terms, the answer could mean the difference in your business' success both now and in the future.

When posed this question recently, one of my clients discovered that few if any of their managers would likely line up with them. The realization was devastating. The answer was that their team simply had gotten lazy. Things had been good, and everyone had apparently become satisfied. The result was that two of the key players in their executive team were replaced. This business owner changed things overnight.

So be very aware that these two questions may be the difference between surviving and thriving.

1. **Who on my team is working for a paycheck?** Who is just getting by? Who is only showing up for work and going home? When you know the answer to this, you at least will know what to expect and where your planning for the future should be focused.

2. **Who on my team is "riding for the brand?"** Who really enjoys their work and is working here specifically because they love their job? Who will go to battle with me when we need to do so? When you know this answer you'll know what moves might be appropriate for you to make to reach your goals and visions for this year and the future. Changes might need to be made!

The honest answer may surprise you. But understand

this . . . to even have a chance at the future you must know the answer.

Survive or Thrive! It's Your Choice!

I am privileged to currently work with clients from all over the world. And, I am blessed with the success that my coaching clients have experienced. But I'll let you in on a little secret—I learn as much from my clients as they learn from me.

The most recent and major reality that I've come to understand is that the issues, needs, challenges, and concerns that businesspeople experience, no matter where they are at in the world, are all basically the same. These issues always seem to revolve around three things: productivity, profitability, and a struggle to improve the quality of their life. However, with the ongoing international economic issues and changing consumer attitudes how we achieve these things has dramatically changed.

I've concluded that there are only two types of business strategies most business owners and managers employ. The most prominent strategy by far is one that is fear-based and works from the simple premise of survival. Here's a great example. I was told by a new customer that his daily goal was to go to work and break even! The battle is already lost with this kind of survival thinking unless we can make a quick and profound change in that thinking. The smaller percentage of business owners and managers have the highest success rate. These are business owners and managers who work from a mindset based on thriving. They strive to take advantage of every opportunity and every situation.

I have compiled a list of the key mindsets that an

entrepreneurial business owner must have and maintain so that they don't merely survive but thrive in this and any economy.

1. **If you conduct business the way you've always done business, you WILL be out of business.** You must adapt, adjust, and change to the changing market and changing customers' attitudes. You must meet their needs from THEIR point of view not what you think they want. Many researchers say that everything we know today will be obsolete in less than two years. Things are changing, and changing fast, so you must too. You cannot afford to be stuck in "the way we've always done it" syndrome.

2. **You must run your business like you did when you started it . . . every day.** In other words, no matter how long you've been in business, you must run it like a "bootstrap" startup, every day. That means you must get back to watching your expenses every day. You must have effective marketing with systems in place to track their effectiveness. Then, when you know the approach isn't working you can, with gusto, STOP it! Everything you do, every penny you spend must have a positive effect. This is really the number one response I've gotten from business development experts when asked about the single most effective trait of successful businesspeople, in any economy wherever they're at in the world.

3. **You must be disciplined.** You must plan and prioritize your time every day! You must read your goals, every day. Be disciplined and do what you need to do, when you need to do it, whether you want to or not. It will make a difference.

4. **Your strategies must be based on WHAT IS vs. WHAT IF.** Understand the reality of the business situations and challenges you face and base your true strategies on those. Slow down, calm down, and understand what's real and what isn't, then create a plan based on facts not possible negative futures.

5. **You must be passionate about what you're doing.** You must enjoy what you're doing even when times are tough and challenging. If you don't, life is quite a bit harder. When you don't have passion for your work, you might just as well quit and put yourself out of your misery. Love what you're doing and your attitude changes—really everything changes for the better. You find yourself looking for opportunities, not problems.

6. **You must work, REALLY, REALLY, REALLY, REALLY, REALLY, REALLY, hard.** Sometimes the answer is so simple that you talk yourself out of it. You can plan for weeks and months, you can worry till you're sick, but nothing happens until you go to work. Right or wrong, the only way to find out, is to go to work. Go to work with a plan, with goals, with enthusiasm and passion. If you can be one of the few who do this, you cannot fail.

7. **REPEAT RULE 6.** Got it? Good!

Your Business Playbook

I use a set of simple rules that applies to all clients no matter what business they're in. I call it my "Business Playbook." Just like a successful football coach has a playbook that houses all strategies and tactics to help them achieve a winning season, we use a Business Playbook. Every few months, you want to bring out the Business Playbook to ask key questions. I always start by asking my clients to set aside three hours or so, slow down, take a deep breath and ask themselves, "How have I done so far this year, really?"

   a. What do I need to do to finish the year strong?

   b. What changes need to be made as soon as possible?

So here, once again, is the basic checklist that I ask everyone to use to evaluate where they're at in their business and in their outlook. Some of these things will take some work. The key is to be honest and, if the answer applies, accept it and get to work. Here we go:

1. Do you know exactly where you're at with your goals? If you don't yet have goals, there's still time. This is key.

2. Take your ego out of the picture. What mistakes have you made? How can you prevent them from happening again?

3. Do you understand what changes and adjustments specifically need to be made? Don't form a committee to discover what went wrong, don't beat anyone up . . . understand the issues then create a solution(s). Then move forward.

4. As an accountability check, were you honest with yourself in working on #3? Make the hard changes now and don't delay. Every minute of delay means lost income and opportunity.

5. Begin to start forming ideas for your next steps. Begin to lay your implementation strategy out. Honesty about what's happened so far is essential for laying out a clear

and powerful plan.

6. If necessary, find a new level of belief in yourself. If you're a bit down, if you've let things get to you, now is the time for a private gut check. No matter the odds or naysayers, you must believe in yourself! If you don't believe in yourself, how can you expect family, customers, employees, bankers, or investors to believe in you?

7. It may sound trite, but are you staying positive minded? Instead of giving yourself reasons why you can't, give yourself reasons why you can! As the great Zig Ziglar once said, "Stop your stinkin' thinkin' and give yourself a check-up from the neck-up!"

8. Be sure now, more than ever, that you ARE doing the most important things you should be doing every day to achieve your goals. Make a new commitment to **time management.** Don't waste a minute of time and never let the least important things take precedence over the most important things.

9. Understand that sometimes being a great leader means having the nerve to say NO! Don't get so busy that you just rubber-stamp every issue, need, problem, or challenge. If you need a little time to make a better decision, take it. Say *no* and instantly control the noise.

10. Are you sure that you strive to treat each day like your first day in business? Are you always focusing on results? Do you continually watch expenses, and make every dollar count?

11. Are you living by the rule to never waste a dime on marketing? Do all the marketing that you can afford, but

do it smart. A few simple rules to follow include creating a tracking and metrics system so you can clearly see if your marketing is or isn't working. If you know it isn't working, **now stop doing it.** Save the budget for other opportunities. Another rule is to be careful not to waste dollars jumping on the bandwagon of the latest social media fad. Check it out and be sure it fits and reaches your target market before leaping in.

12. Are you sure you are flexible enough with your strategic plan? The rule is: If you continue to do business the way you've always done business then you WILL be out of business!

13. Ask yourself, "Am I as disciplined as I need to be?" The rule that applies here is defined by the pure definition of the word *discipline*: Doing what you have to do, when you have to do it, whether you want to or not.

14. Ask yourself, "Am I putting in the time necessary to get the job done?"

15. Are you still passionate about what you're doing? If not, you must stop doing what you're doing and get out of the way . . . for your own good and those around you. If necessary, make the changes now and start fresh.

This is just part of my Crunchtime Checklist. More of the checklist will follow, but I hope by now that you get the picture. Be diligent about continuous improvement. Yes, these checklist items are basic, but I challenge you to honestly answer each question. It's hard, but necessary to the point that it could mean your complete success or failure, your surviving or thriving, and be a major step in the position that you now will have the power to put yourself in.

Problem Solving? No Problem!

Sometimes all the motivational mantras in the world still are not enough to make you feel better. When you have a problem, a big one, a real whopper, the last thing you need is to have someone say, "Problems are just veiled opportunities" or "There are no problems, only solutions." Even though I have said these things myself, sometimes they're just not enough.

When we have a problem, it's uncomfortable, it doesn't feel good, and sometimes dealing with it can be physically debilitating. The fact is, most businesspeople are not equipped to handle problems of any kind. It's a skill that isn't taught. The skill of effective problem solving is a learned skill and a skill that I believe to be essential to long-term survival and growth, both personally and professionally.

I have found that there are effective and foundational methods to help you with problem-solving. The one that I've found most effective is a four-step process that's easy to implement because it's easy to remember. The hard part is just facing up to the process and doing it.

First, let's set the scene.

You must find some solitude. Step back and find somewhere where you can sit quietly for thirty minutes. Get away from the mob and manage the noise. If it helps, listen to music, but make it classical music. Studies show that soft, instrumental (no vocals) music playing while you're problem-solving aids in the process. It relaxes the mind allowing it to be more receptive to free and creative thinking.

Sit down now with a pad of paper. Write at the top of the pad your problem or situation. Be very, very specific about the issue, because the more complete and total clarity you have, the odds grow for getting a quick solution.

So now the four MAGIC steps in making problem solving easy!

Write down these three questions, then answer write your answers down quickly and without hesitation.

STEP 1: **Ask yourself, "What happened, really?** "What happened to cause this situation? Be honest—what really happened?

STEP 2: **Now, ask yourself, "Why did this happen?"** What were the circumstances behind the issue? What caused the situation in the first place? Again, be honest no matter how it may hurt.

STEP 3: **Next, ask yourself, "What can I do so that this never happens again?"** What are the things I can do, actions I can take, changes and adjustments that can be made so this situation never happens again?

STEP 4: **Put the issue in the rearview mirror!** Literally hold your arm up in the air, turn your wrist so your hand is pointing backward and ceremonially wave bye-bye to the issue! If you learned anything and applied what you learned, then you can simply forget about the issue completely, knowing with confidence that the issue will never happen again, but if it does, you know what you need to do to squash it immediately.

It's all about learning from the problems and issues we face in life. Use this system and leave all the anger, frustration, blame, and indigestion to someone else. All that can be damaging to your health and can be costly. Remember:

1. What happened?

2. Why did it happen?

3. How will it never happen again?

4. Bye-bye

Now that your problems are solved, go take a nap, or even better, go sell something!

The Art of Hiring Telecommuting Employees

Employers are looking more and more for future employees and managers and leaders with the skills to telecommute. Today about fifty percent of the U.S. workforce holds a job that is compatible with at least partial telework and approximately twenty-five percent of the workforce teleworks at some frequency. And the numbers are growing for good reason. The economic potential is staggering. Businesses that promote telecommuting see almost instant growth in their productivity and reduced absenteeism and turnover. For most business owners, it is always amazing how much work someone can get done when you eliminate the "drive-by" co-worker who hangs around to chat about last night's game or how lousy the weather is. In fact, the opportunity to telecommute is now considered a perk by many employees and with that then comes higher job satisfaction and improved work-life balance.

Global Workplace Analytics projects that businesses in the United States alone could save (you might want to sit down) $500 billion a year with a telecommuting program. The savings come from the reduction of utilities, janitorial services, security, maintenance, coffee and water, parking, furniture, office supplies, and office space.

So far, telecommuting sounds all fine and dandy, but

there is a dark side to telecommuting that every company that considers it should take into consideration. Not every employee has the skills and discipline to telecommute. Several years ago, when the idea of telecommuting was just catching on, I was a National Sales Manager for a company that thought it would be very cutting-edge to allow all our salespeople the perk of working from home. We quickly learned that we shouldn't have made that move. Some of our top sales producers who thrived in a team environment and an office-centered sales base, ended up, after a month at home, in their underwear, eating potato chips and watching ESPN every afternoon. Their past success was based on the accountability that going to the office represented.

A company that is considering telecommuting must be selective in who gets this perk. The only way productivity grows, and job satisfaction increases if the employee possesses certain competencies and skills to make it work. Some of those would include:

Self-discipline: When they get up in the morning, do they have the discipline to then go into the next room and get to work?

Self-Management: Can they manage time and priorities without a supervisor looking over their shoulder?

Focus: Can the employee focus on the task at hand and not be easily distracted by email, video games, kids, dogs, telephone chats, TV, naps, ESPN, etc.?

Communication Skills: Can the employee effectively communicate as good as or better than they might in the corporate office setting? Can they build a relationship with customers and prospects in any business setting?

Tech Savvy: An employee must be able to understand and utilize all the tools that are necessary to do their job and communicate clearly. If they're lost with technology, they're frustrated—and if they're frustrated, they aren't working.

Telecommuting is more than a fad and a money-saving convenience, it's becoming necessary for many companies to offer in order to attract the best talent. If you're a business owner, get a plan in place to screen, train, and deploy your people. If you're an employee, hone your self-discipline and self-management skills and you might have a competency that top companies are looking for.

Has Anyone Seen your Website?

I probably need to clarify something before I get much farther. I am, for the most part, technologically feeble even though I've spent most of my life working in and with technology in some form. The truth be told, of the fourteen start-ups I've been a part of, at least ten of them were technology/IT start-ups. I'm an idea guy, a sales and marketing trailblazer, so I've always surrounded myself with people far more qualified than myself in technology. Then I focused on the sales and marketing side. And that, my dear friends, is what this chapter is all about.

I'm not here to tell you how to improve your website and get it seen based on the technical stuff. I have friends and clients who are virtual experts about that side of the equation. What I want you to do is to look at your website and forget about the technical stuff (stuff is such a nice technical word, right?). Today we're discussing the other things that make a website great. These things include the look and feel, the marketing and sales elements. These are the things that will keep your internet-based customers on your site once they get there, for longer periods of time. Although experts can take you through an entire litany of different strategies and applications, I want to focus on just eight of what I believe are among the most important. These are a few of the key elements that we would discuss in a business coaching session if you were sitting with me. So here we go.

1. **Generic Is Not Allowed:** If you're in business and you have a website for your business, GENERIC is not a word that should exist in your vocabulary. You cannot afford to spend a dime today on generic advertising or marketing, and that includes your website. You had better be using it for powerful validation; to generate more traffic; to help current customers and build future customers by providing specific benefits; to provide specific solutions; and to show specific value and to present specific offers and opportunities.

2. **Use Headlines:** Remember the newspaper? How did or do you read the newspaper? Everyone reads the paper pretty much the same way, anywhere in the world. And just like they read the newspaper, research is showing they read internet news sites and newsletters the same way— they read the headlines first. Always! So be sure your website isn't overloaded with text. Break it down into big headlines and smaller headlines to attract interest and keep visitors reading.

3. **Use White Space:** Another technique from the newspaper industry. A great ad in the paper, if you talk with the pros, is not one that's just a page or a space with wall-to-wall words. Leave some open or white space. Give the

headlines room to work. The exercise of creating white space is a good one, in that it challenges you to only include the information that really makes a difference in attracting and transforming a casual reader into a customer.

4. **Always Have a Specific Call-to-Action:** Always, always, always ask your web customers to do or respond to something, anything worthwhile. Have them click to go to a page to fill in their information and request a white paper; obtain research; to get an online coupon; to sign up for a free class; to sign up for a newsletter . . . ASK THEM TO DO SOMETHING! If they're visiting your site, it's your responsibility to capture their email, phone number, and anything else you can, to build a powerful database. But always, always, always have a call to action throughout your site.

5. **Answer the Two Key Questions of Marketing:** This is one of the biggest mistakes I see when working with my clients. The two key questions of marketing are not scientific, but they are universal. The questions are the phrase, "so what?" and "WIIFM" or "What's in It for Me?" Just remember to ask yourself those two questions with every paragraph you write or every offer you make to your readers. Why? Because those two questions are asked by every single one of your readers, prospects, and customers as they read every paragraph or offer you have. They're saying, "So what? What does this have to do with me and my business and how can it help?" If you don't answer those two questions every time, you're sunk. So, practice implementing these acid-test questions immediately and the effectiveness of your articles and

your offers should double overnight.

6. **It's Not About You!** Often, business owners will build their website and when it's complete it looks like a shrine to the business owner. There is a place for a bio and some achievements, but a great business website is designed to promote your business and answer the "so what?" and "WIIFM" question for the reader. So be sure your site is full of benefits, features, and successes of the business.

7. **Become Friends with a Font:** Gads, this one really gripes me. Don't get caught up in trying to be cute with your look and feel. Find a nice businesslike font that you like and use it consistently throughout your site. It makes a huge difference in readability.

8. **Ditto with Colors:** The same rules apply as in point 7. Be sure you find colors that look good, aren't too garish, and make sense for your business. Again, many people try to be cute with bright colors and cute 3-D type background colors. What they end up with is a color scheme where you simply cannot read the content . . . and potential clients and buyers have got to be able to read your content. So, scrutinize your site and test all its functions as thoroughly as possible. Ask a graphic design pro what they think, then find a color or combination and stick with it. Color is a great tool for creating an impression and image.

I hope this helps. Just remember that there is more to the success of a business website than paying for the backend technology which makes it run—that's just half the equation. The presentation is what makes you money, so be sure to get it right and put it to work for you!

**Go here for your
Monthly/Quarterly Business Review Checklist:**

businesscoachdan.com/straighttalk

Part
8

Marketing

How to Screw Up and Waste Money on Marketing

Most marketing plans totally suck! They are destined for failure simply because they are based on facts and figures that simply don't apply to a successful marketing campaign.

I subscribe to over forty newsletters on business, sales, marketing, and such, just so I can make a feeble attempt to keep up with the "speed of light" changes that are happening in the marketplace. One of the biggest areas of change that is taking place is in marketing. I would guess that millions of marketing dollars are literally going down the toilet every day due to changes in marketing that cause mistakes to be made.

Advertising guru, David Ogilvy, once famously said, "50% of all advertising budgets are wasted. The problem is we don't know which 50%." One thing I know is that something can be done about advertising to give you an edge. I am a firm believer that for any strategy to work, the foundational elements of success must be in place.

I recently came across an article by Mr. Geoffrey James who writes for *Inc.com*. I had to laugh, as it seems Geoffrey and I have faced many of the same issues. The article was his view of the common marketing mistakes that businesspeople make. Like Mr. James, I, too, have viewed thousands of marketing plans and strategies and most of them smell worse than old tennis shoes. Most of them are terrible. When you don't have the basics down, what you end up with is an award-winning and creative advertising campaign that doesn't sell anything. I recently had a client tell me that their problems with advertising were over. He had just spent a ton of money on a new, award-laden with the belief this would solve all his problems. I asked him a couple of questions about his business. When the deafening silence lifted, he fired the copywriter and went to work getting answers to some questions that are the key to avoiding marketing issues. So, with a nod to Mr. James article here is a version of what I believe will help businesses avoid wasting money.

The 5 Most Common Marketing Mistakes

1. **No Idea Who the Ideal Customer Is.** I ask you this: How in the world can you create any kind of marketing plan or campaign, write any kind of sales copy for radio, TV, magazine, or newspaper if you have no idea who to target? Wake up and smell the cappuccino people, the days of mass "shotgun" marketing are over. There are too many outlets and too many channels. If you continue to market your business the way you've always marketed your business, you may soon be out of business. Know who your customer is and don't spend another dime on marketing until you do. Dig a bit, find the truth. Do not assume who your target customer is, just because that's who it's always been. Find out. Go through your client records and build a profile. Watch who walks through your door, or who is calling. Who specifically is your perfect target consumer and how do they acquire their information? You can't afford to guess at this anymore.

2. **No Idea What the Ideal Customer Wants.** If you're lucky enough to fully understand who your customer or customers are, the question is this: do you really know what they want? That requires listening, asking, and understanding. Basic demographic and market research do not accomplish this. You need to look them in the eye and ask them what they want and what you need to do to get them to come to your store or buy your

service, versus buying the same product from fifty other businesses selling your product or service online. In other words, understand the customer's needs from the customer's point of view.

3. **No Idea as to What Business You're Really In.** In a classic example, when railroads around North America began to fail, the owners were asked what business they were in and they proudly stated they were in the railroad business. When in fact, due to changes in our world, they were really in the transportation business. This one paradigm change contributed to changing the entire industry. Is a realtor someone who sells houses? Or, is a realtor someone who helps families make the biggest financial decision they may ever make? This one adjustment, to know more clearly what business you are really in and why you are in it, will improve the clarity of your marketing message instantly.

4. **No Idea Why Anyone Should Buy or What Sets You Apart from the Competition.** It is imperative to sit down and clearly understand your UNIQUE VALUE PROPOSITION, or why a prospect should buy from you versus your competition. It's just as important to understand precisely why a client should *continue* to buy from you. How do you expect your marketing to work without this information? The answer is, it won't.

5. **No Idea How to Explain Your Business in Thirty Seconds or Less.** Most of us have experienced the pain of going to a networking event where everyone gets a chance to tell their "story" and ninety-nine percent of the room stumbles and stutters and rambles on and on, and after tap dancing for thirty or sixty seconds the audience

still doesn't know what business the speaker is in. A good succinct marketing message isn't just helpful at networking meetings, it's imperative for your marketing as well. The key is in giving a concise explanation of your "why." Why do you do what you do? For example: "I help people to truly love their homes" is much more powerful than, "I'm a decorator." Take some time and work on refining your message and get some help if you need to.

The key to marketing is to kick aside the standard responses and let people really know that you're passionate about what you do and that you want their business. If you can't do that, you will be replaced by someone who can succinctly speak their "why."

Who is your IDEAL Customer, Really?

Do you know your ideal client . . . even when you see them? The fact that most business owners do not get, is that your *ideal* client is much different from your *typical* client. Your typical client *needs* what you sell, but your ideal client *wants* what you sell! That difference is huge. Prospects may or may not buy what they need, but they always buy what they want. If you know how to find your ideal client, you can literally dominate your market. But again, the fact of the matter is, if you don't know who they are and what they look like, you can *never* find them!

It sounds incredible really, but I see this, literally every day. Thousands of dollars of marketing budgets and lost time go out the window because the businessperson has no idea who their customer really is or what their customer really needs, and just as importantly, who their customer has evolved to become. Let me give you a couple of examples. One client proudly said they had just hired an award-winning copywriter so their media copy would be powerful, funny, and award-winning. This was much better copy than what they had previously had, and my client really believed that great copy would help him find success with his marketing.

Unfortunately, I rained on his parade with this one question: "Who is your target customer?" He could answer in general but without any specifics. It became quickly easy to see that without knowing who his target customer was, how they thought, how and why they bought, and what they wanted, the best copywriter in the world could not write effective copy that got results. They might win some advertising awards, but without achieving results. It was essential for the copywriter to know who to target the message to!

Remember this, prospects buy, based on emotions, and wants are *emotion based*. Needs are *logic based*. When your product or service matches what your prospects specifically want, you will immediately begin to attract your ideal client. So, take some time to come up with your answers. Slow down and take a long hard look at how your business has evolved, do some research, tap into some industry information and then, if necessary, re-configure who you sell to and what you sell them. You'll be happy . . . and your customers will be happier!

Everyone Buys Toilet Paper

Several years ago, I came to understand that the act of buying toilet paper was a major lesson in the art of being a good businessman and a great marketer. Crazy, right? Who would have ever thought?

I can honestly say the lesson here was one of the great insights I have learned on my professional path to high-level marketing and sales success.

The thinking goes like this: "You'll never be a great marketing or sales professional until you realize that when you go home, at some point, you'll need to go buy toilet paper too!"

Translation: At some point in time, we all are consumers, every one of us. The lesson is that in order to be really, really good at marketing and sales, we must also remember we are also consumers. Which in application means that we must learn to critique any marketing materials, advertising copy, or sales scripts as both the marketer and the consumer.

We create these materials (or pay someone to create them) with the intent to use them to sell our product or service to prospective consumers. But the difference in good copy that wins awards and copy that really entices the consumer to buy, is usually a result of applying the true "acid" test.

The acid test is simply the act of stepping back, putting on your consumer hat and critically looking at the material you've just written or created, then asking yourself, "Would I buy that?" If you, as the consumer say *no*, then you should accept the fact that the message isn't strong enough and go immediately back to the drawing board. If it's cute or funny but doesn't really sell your product, admit it and start over.

It's such a simple act, but it's amazing how few businesspeople, marketers, sales professionals and the like, do not use this powerful technique. There are some variations on the question that include:

- "Would I buy that?" Simply put, do you get the value

proposition? Does the offer make the sense? Be honest!

- "So what?" Just look at the material and if the words "so what" come to mind, you need to start over. Read the material a couple of times. If the material makes you laugh but on the second reading you find yourself thinking, *so what*, then it's time to work on it again.

- "WII-FM" (What's in It for Me?) If you now catch yourself saying "So what? What's in it for me?", then you really need to step back and start afresh. Great copy or sales material should never leave a doubt about what is being sold and the value to the consumer.

The bottom line is that without these simple checks and balances you could waste a ton of budget on marketing and sales materials that don't work . . . and they don't work because they don't relate to what the consumer wants. This can all be avoided if you just remember that you, too, are a consumer.

I hope this simple thought helps you on your personal and business growth journey. I must stop writing now. I have to go to the store—I hear toilet paper is on sale!

One Simple Secret to Improve Your Business

We all know someone who spends their life worrying and struggling and always "fighting fires" (problems and emergencies). They live a *reactive* life, not a *proactive* life. Then, when there are no fires to fight, they become anxious and fearful, afraid they're doing something wrong. They then sabotage themselves by creating fires to fight, simply so they have something to do and something to complain about.

I work daily with executives and affluent business owners

and am constantly amazed at how totally off track and out of alignment they can get by chasing rainbows and "silver bullet" solutions to improve their life and their business, or both. Miracle cures seldom work in life or business. By now, you've learned that I practice and preach the gospel of basics. In almost all cases where I am working with a struggling executive or businessperson, the cause of the struggle is usually in the fact that the client has slipped away from applying many of the basic success principles that they already know. So, it is usually my challenge to look for viable alternatives that revolve around time-proven principles or foundational applications and strategies that must be in place before anything fancy can ever work. The solution that is seldom chosen is to just slow down and believe that there might be a better way to address the issue that makes sense and can solve the problem immediately, with an easy approach to implementation.

There are a couple of good examples that I personally use and encourage my clients to use. These are simple and logical. The primary and the simplest secret of improving your business is to remember this one statement:

**Not all consumers are businesspeople,
but all businesspeople are consumers!**

I have been privileged to have some great mentors in my life and one of them, an exceedingly wise business person, would drill this into me: "You will be a great businessman someday only if you remember that when you go home every night, you have to go out and buy (toilet paper) groceries too!"

The truth in both statements is that businesspeople everywhere need to train themselves to be able to analyze their business offers, advertising, marketing, proposals, displays, communications, and every element of doing business with the "eye of the consumer." Remember that as a consumer, we make value decisions all the time on where we choose to purchase and why we buy. Those decisions are usually made based on what is said, the offer, the presentation or the look, taste or feel that the business creates and represents. In turn, why shouldn't we take this same evaluation and apply it to every piece of our own business communication and simply ask ourselves, "If I was considering purchasing from this person/business, would I move forward with the purchase?" Or, "Is this offer something that entices me to do business with this person?" Yes, you're looking at your own offers, scripts, and materials, but if your inner consumer answers the questions with a *no*, then you better head back to the old drawing board. Go back again and again until your answer changes.

This is a powerful yet simple exercise that costs you nothing to do but can save you money and make you money. You simply need to have the ability to honestly criticize your own business communication, looking at it as an unbiased consumer.

The key is in how honest you can be in critiquing your own work. The answer to that will be the difference in consistent and ongoing improvement for your business . . . or not! Take the time and do this now.

Go here for your Business Marketing Checklist:

businesscoachdan.com/straighttalk

Part
9 • • • • • • •

Succession
Planning

Time to Retire? Not Yet.
Five Tips for Sustainable Succession Planning

I have had many clients who, after successfully starting and running their business, felt like the time had come where they were ready to go sit on a beach somewhere, but soon realized that getting out of the business wasn't as easy as they thought it might be. They thought they could just sell it or pass it on to family or employees. The decision and the process is never easy. There is work to be done to accomplish this goal. And, this is where most business owners struggle. They don't know the process because they've never considered the process until now.

I force all my clients, to write a business plan, or update their current business plan to include an exit strategy. My concern is always that by being unprepared to exit, there will always be money left on the table. Sometimes the money left behind can be substantial!

I'm always doing research of some kind and while looking for information on exit planning, I found an article by Mr. Adam Wong to be very timely. Repeatedly, I work with business owners who have dedicated a lifetime to their business with absolutely no consideration to the future of their business when they decide to retire. Here you'll find five superb thoughts for preparing for the future. Read, learn, and apply.

Successful Succession Planning

According to the 2012 Chief Executive study by Booz & Company, of the world's largest 2,500 public companies, fifteen percent of CEOs were replaced last year, and seventy-two percent of CEO turnovers were actually planned successions, suggesting that companies are working more thoughtfully than ever to ensure they put in place new leaders who will best serve the company for years to come.

Consider the senior leadership of your organization. Has your company made plans for the transition of these individuals? Succession planning is least effective when it is developed on an as-needed basis (in fact, it really should be called "crisis management" in that case). Instead, succession planning should be ingrained in your complete talent-management plan, making it a part of the way you do business. With every new hire you make, and as you onboard each employee, there are simple ways you can ensure their skills and experience can withstand the inevitable changes that lie ahead.

Benchmark every position. Succession planning should originate in the role-definition process. It is there that stakeholders begin to truly understand the traits necessary for success in the role.

Don't just hire for now. If you hire for now, you may miss the candidate who can flourish in the future. Picture each candidate in future roles within the company.

Be candid throughout the interview process. As much as you are interviewing candidates to better understand if they will fit into the culture of your organization, those candidates are interviewing you. Listen for their desires to grow within your company.

Instill the question, "What's next?" Don't wait for new employees to become acclimated to their jobs to intentionally communicate the company's plans for growth. When you start having these conversations from day one, your "A players" will subscribe to your vision and will see themselves in the company's growth plan.

Don't assume all employees desire the same things. Just because you see leadership potential in an individual doesn't mean he or she shares in that desire for growth. Make sure those employees are comfortable in positions that are more constant and continue to communicate with those individuals in case their desires change.

When you are operating with a sustainable succession plan, you will be able to look ahead and identify any gaps before they can affect the company. And, as you are identifying high potentials within the organization, you'll be able to adjust each person's development process to suit the critical needs of the company.

> ### Go here to get your
> ### Exit/Succession Planning Guidance Sheet
> businesscoachdan.com/straighttalk

Part 10

Setting Goals & Achieving Them

A Leap of Faith

The most powerful secret of all consistent goal achievers, people who exceed all expectations, the top two percent in whatever field they're in, is in the mastery of one simple question!

"If I knew I could not fail, how big would I allow myself to dream?"

Be honest! Ask yourself how much your current thinking might change if you KNEW you could not fail! If you could eliminate all restrictions AND constraints on your success, how much additional confidence might you have? Your answer to this question is critical to your future. Many entrepreneurs and businesspeople have an innate lack of confidence. They will over analyze opportunities to a point of making bad decisions. I ask this question to every client that I work with, in my business coaching practice, and I never cease to be amazed at some of the answers I get. Even when I remind the client that it's just an exercise and we're just playing the *"what if"* game, many will balk. When I emphatically make the point that all constraints would be removed, that success would be guaranteed if they just moved forward, I still get looks of fear and anxiety and a distinct lack of confidence.

This question works at several levels. On one hand, it is a test of your faith, faith in yourself; faith in your business; faith in your idea. Just how passionate are you? How willing are you to have a vision and stand by it and pursue it no matter what the obstacles might be? On another level, the question can be a benchmark for someone who is considering pursuing a business or product idea. I guarantee you that based on your answer; you can measure your chances for success or failure! Which brings us to the reality, that this question can expose an inherent fear of failure. Regina Dugan directs the Defense Advanced Research Projects Agency (DARPA), where their entire business plan and its success or failure is based on asking "The Question." Dugan summarizes the process by saying, "I'm not encouraging failure. I am discouraging the fear of failure." "Fear of failure constrains us, and amazing things STOP happening." She goes on to say, "Remove the fear of failure, and impossible things, suddenly become possible. The fear of failure constrains us, and it keeps us from attempting great things!"

In research conducted by a major university, a large sample group of entrepreneurs were studied in the effort to find out what the key contributing factors were to be a successful entrepreneur and businessperson. The results were nothing short of remarkable. Age did not matter; Income did not matter; title did not matter; gender, heritage, ethnicity, education, and experience were not significant contributing factors. In fact, there was only one primary similarity that they all shared... just one. The trait that was found to be inherent to successful entrepreneurs, was simply the willingness to (at some point) step out in faith! This means that every one of these people had decided when enough research and planning had been done. Enough worry and investigation and training had been completed. That whether they were completely ready or not, it was time to launch, to step out and begin their journey. To dive in and go through the process of failing, learning, adjusting and then do it again.

They had indeed asked and answered the question, *"If*

you knew you could not fail, how big would you allow yourself to dream?" In doing so, they allowed themselves to dream and imagine the possibilities, and in that process, learning that more was possible than they ever would have imagined prior to asking the question.

Think about how different our world might be if not a single person was willing to allow their selves to dream. In 1895 Lord Kelvin proclaimed that "heavier than air flying machines were impossible!" In 1904, Ferdinand Foch, a revered French Army General said, "Airplanes are interesting toys but of no military value!" Yet in a relatively short span of time, on October 14, 1947, Chuck Yeager flew faster than the speed of sound! Auto maker and entrepreneur extraordinaire, Henry Ford was said to have commented that, *"If I had asked people what they wanted, they would have said a faster horse."* The act of thinking, of thinking big, without restrictions or constraints and then allowing dreams to happen, has consistently changed mankind!

Force yourself this week to accomplish this one action item. Ask yourself The Question. Don't analyze or pre-judge on whether your answers are possible or even probable. That's not the purpose of this exercise. How big can you ALLOW yourself to dream? That's the question. Have some fun! Who knows, you may surprise yourself and change the world . . . your world at least!

Part 11

Clarity = Success

Clarity is a Game Changer!

When you walk into my office, you will find that the top third of all my whiteboards have one word highlighted: CLARITY. One of the consistent reasons why a business or person succeeds or fails is that they have either an abundance of, or a distinct lack of, foundational clarity. The great thing is, it's totally up to each individual and business which situation we choose to live in.

There was a time when we could get away with a lack of clarity. But in today's business world, clarity will help you get the specific customers you want, define your purpose, and help you claim rich dividends. For instance, if you want to sell red wagons, who is going to be your target audience? You need clarity to figure that out so you can zoom into the exact customer profile. Will young parents with little kids like Red Wagons or will people over seventy-five like Red Wagons?

Clarity makes you understand the customers' needs based on the customers' point of view. This attitude changes everything. When we learn to understand needs from another person's point of view, this means we're solving needs and issues by what the customer or prospect believes them to be, not what we believe them to be. This one simple mindset forces us to be better listeners. If we just shut the heck up and listen, our prospects and clients WILL tell us how to help them and how to sell them.

Here is an example of something that happened recently. There was (and I emphasize the word, *was*) a hardware store whose owners decided they would dedicate a substantial portion of their store to flooring, carpeting, tile, and home accessories. This decision was based totally on their vision for what they thought the neighborhood wanted. Not long ago, this store closed. You must wonder if anyone in an upper-income neighborhood would ever want to tell their friends that they remodeled their half-million-dollar home through a neighborhood hardware store? Most people go to the neighborhood hardware store to buy items for immediate needs. Was this business trying to be something that they wanted, or was sufficient research done to justify that this is what the neighborhood wanted? We'll never know for sure, but I would bet that more CLARITY would have helped.

In scenarios like these, CLARITY matters. Clarity of purpose will help us create a product or service based on our customers' point of view and not our point of view. There are numerous examples of businesses that have failed because of a lack of clarity. Just take the case of the healthcare.gov website controversy we had a few years ago. Why did this seemingly great idea initially fail? The reason is simple: people who designed the healthcare.gov site failed to ask clear questions of their users. They never asked the users exactly what it was that they needed. They didn't ask the users how they could build the site to be the easiest to use with the clearest instructions. They never explained to the user just exactly why there was a need for so many forms and so many choices. They never asked the user for input on how to simplify the process so that any user, even those with less education, could easily navigate the site. No, some wonky, chuckle-head bureaucrat with a big title decided that his development department had the expertise to determine what the consumer wanted without needing to ask them.

The first step to understanding clarity regarding your business is to ask questions. The more we ask, we more information we will acquire, and this can help us focus on where we want to go.

Clarity also leads us to accountability and helps us keep a tab on our progress. In my office I have business plans of enterprises I started decades ago. Whether anyone sees them or not, well-done, honest, business plans force you to ask yourself questions that will clarify your vision, sometimes allowing you to see new opportunities and, in turn, pitfalls. When I went through unchartered waters, my business plan was a fabulous tool as reference.

Do not be afraid of CLARITY. Yes, if you've allowed yourself to answer the tough questions with easy answers, you should be afraid of clarity. But if you have the guts to ask, research, listen and follow the clarity that you achieve, your life and your business will most assuredly change. And just to be clear, you can never have enough clarity! I have a mentor who taught me a great lesson about clarity. He would ask me a challenging question. After taking the time to give his question honest, tough reflection and hard-core thinking, I would come up with an answer that I was sure would not only win his approval but win me a Nobel Prize for Great Answers. I would sit with him again and proudly share my revelation. He would look at me with a twinkle in his eye and gruffness in his speech. Then he would calmly say, "What else?" I could not believe it when he said that! What did he mean, "What else?" I had used up a couple years of brain power to come up with my award-winning answer. What else? Really!

And then, just as quickly, I got it. It was just a challenge to me, asking me if I had really thought of everything, every possibility. In today's rapidly changing technological environment, last week could be the distant past. So now, no matter how sure I am about my thoughts and decisions, whether it's for building my own business or working with a client, I always, stop and ask, "What else?"

Let's pursue our tasks with perseverance and crystal-clear clarity. Make sure you have your goals clearly in front of you always so you can see the pathway to even greater success.

Straight ..... **Talk**™

For full information on booking Dan Creed
for personal or professional business coaching,
or to speak at your next meeting,
please visit www.realworldbusinesscoach.com
or call us directly at (602) 697-5949

CHAMPIONS
NEVER MAKE
COLD CALLS

High-Impact
Low-Cost
Lead Generation

DANNY CREED

The Fail-Proof System

Champions'

*"All businesses are about three things: skills, doors, and **Champions**. The doors open and they will open on occasion for any business coach. A **Champion** will help open those doors for you, or they're on the other side of the door and they open it and let you in. But a **Champion** is not interested in anyone without formidable skills. So, a Business Coach can only really effectively advance their interests by getting skillful, and then they get recognized hopefully by a **Champion** who will help them open doors."*

Network

™

PARAPHRASED FROM A QUOTE BY PAT FRALEY,
ADAPTED BY BUSINESS COACH DAN CREED

Welcome to the Champions' Power Referral Network. I devised the process and strategy behind this system through years of trial and error and frustration. Like anyone who has ever sold anything, we know that prospects and customers just do not fall from a tree. They come from lots of hard work and sometimes (particularly in the past) lots of cold calling. Great prospects and new customers also are a product of smart marketing and calculated networking and several other time-intensive activities.

At first, I thought it would be insane to think I could achieve all of these strategies. If I did, how would I have time to sell to the leads that I generated? The problem was obvious, but I didn't know what to do about it. Most of the experts in the field at that time didn't know what to do either. Everyone who taught successful selling seemed to avoid that issue. I read all the books about selling and prospecting, but none pointed me to a simple way to get everything done using one strategy. It made sense to me that a simple strategy to accomplish all the "required" activities was what was needed.

Another thing that made a lot of sense was that the pressure of finding prospects should never be solely on my shoulders. I observed many salespeople struggling, working long hours trying to find qualified prospects. Their success was based on how many of their limited hours they spent in front of prospects.

That is a huge weight for anyone to bear.

A solution came to mind. I decided to focus on how I might build a massive army of "referral" agents—people who either knew me and liked me, respected me, loved me, or simply wanted to help me. People who would readily refer me to others when and if they had a chance.

The challenge to set up a system where this would work not only for me, but for others, was on. This led to years of piecing together the thoughts of some of the top minds in the sales business and adding those to my own experiences. The result of my focus was the development of the Champions' Power Referral Network for lead generation, a system that has proven to be overwhelmingly successful.

I use this system every day. Because I do, I've built a successful, world-class business-coaching practice. It's allowed me to profitably build large sales organizations and I've used it in thirteen entrepreneurial startups. I have taught this system to my local and international sales staff for years. I have trained thousands of professional salespeople to use this system. It was created through a burning desire to change and adjust to the market. Simply put . . .

IT WORKS!
BUT THERE ARE
NO SHORTCUTS!

The concepts of the program are not new. You will have heard about some of the concepts, although some will be fresh. But what the Champions' Power Referral Network does is put the most powerful—and sometimes simple techniques—into one cohesive blueprint. The system encompasses all the secrets of prospecting, networking, marketing, priority/time management skills, and sales strategies that promise to propel those who use them to the top of their field.

RESULTS:

- Since 2007, I have NEVER made a cold call. I know how to do those and I'm good at doing them, but I would rather go to a prospect because I've been recommended by one of their trusted colleagues.

- I average over 150 face-to-face prospect meetings a year, all coming from my Champions' Power Referral Network.

- For more than a decade, every new client I acquire comes from a referral from someone in my Champions' Power Referral Network

- I've stopped going to big, worthless networking meetings where 90% of attendees were not my prospects. I only attend small, focused meetings where 90% of the attendees ARE my prospects. Using my formula, there's little time wasted attending worthless events which gives me more time with my clients and my family.

Champions' Power Referral Network factoid: No matter your profession, to be *successful* you must be a salesperson. And, a successful salesperson is fundamentally a leads-generation expert.

Simply put, show me a struggling business professional and I'll show you a "frustrated and struggling" salesperson. In turn, I'll show you a salesperson who doesn't know how to generate leads or, in many cases, is someone who doesn't want to put the work in that is required to generate leads.

This system proves to work with experienced sales professionals. It also proves to be just as effective for a new salesperson. In addition, it is a simple and phenomenally successful tool for executives who are now, possibly for the first time in their career, required to sell. That's because the Champions' Power Referral Network has proven to be a powerful lead generation system that is ongoing and systematic.

One of the best salespeople I've ever known used to say "Filling the sales funnel was not the hard part. The hard part is keeping the funnel full!" Basically, it's fairly easy to generate a few leads and put them in the sales funnel or pipeline. But cut off the flow of leads and you'll find yourself with *no leads, no prospects, no customers, and no job.*

There are two major benefits of the Champions' Power Referral Network for lead generation. The first is eliminating cold calling.

NEVER, EVER DO ANOTHER COLD CALL!

A major benefit of my system eliminates the age-old bugaboo of every salesperson that has ever existed (whether they admit it or not) and that's generating the energy and the nerve to do cold calls! No one likes cold calling.

And just to be clear, my distaste for the practice starts with the premise that cold calling is the poorest use of a salesperson's time I can imagine. It's random. It's unfocused. It's intrusive . . .and in today's marketplace, intrusive is not welcome.

Your odds are better if you took a week and your life savings and went to Vegas. Think about it. You're randomly contacting hundreds of people who don't know you, don't trust you, and initially don't care who you are or what you want . . .and you're trying to get them to sit down with you so you can tell them why they should talk with you some more.

Cold calling has no doubt been the foundation of many sales organizations of the past and the technique once worked. Today, it is a technique of the past and it isn't an acceptable strategy for the successful salesperson in the challenging market we now face. Why? The market has changed. Technology triggered this change. The constant and rapid advancement of technology has changed consumers (our customers and prospects) and we had better understand just what that means if we want to be successful.

Here's how that's reflected: any information that a customer or prospect wants, they can now get in a matter of seconds through their computer, notepad, or handheld communication device. In fact, some research now suggests that as much as seventy percent of all buying decisions are now made *prior to a first meeting.* So, the whole idea of cold calling has been turned upside down. Basically, this means that when a consumer needs a product or service, they now go straight to their communication device of choice. They Google for the information or resource they need and get an instantaneous list. From this list, they then interview suppliers of the product or service. So, while a salesperson may go into a first meeting and treat it as a "discovery" meeting, the fact is, the prospect sees the meeting as a second meeting because they've already done their research. They will expect you to have done your research as well, dispensing with the traditional questions such as, "So, can you tell me a little about your business?" The prospect of today expects you to have already done that research, just as they have researched you and your competitors.

The change in buying patterns is obvious. Consumers/customers/prospects do not want or need to be cold called. There was a time that worked, but that time is over and the sooner you understand this and apply more accepted techniques, the sooner you will become an effective salesperson in this digital age.

As salespeople, we must look for ways to find prospects who already know what they want and need. We had better be interacting with prospects and clients and sell to them in a way they want to be sold to, not the way we've always done it.

> **Champions'** ... *"Marketing and sales isn't about trying to persuade, coerce or manipulate people into buying your services. It's about putting yourself out in front of, and offering your services to, those whom you are meant to serve, those people who already need and are looking for your services."* **Network** ...

MICHAEL PORT

What the prospect wants today is understanding. UNDERSTANDING! This is the ability to *ask not tell*. This is the ability to work together in a complimentary, "no-pitch" environment where both parties are simply evaluating to see if there are obvious needs one of them have that can be solved by the other person. Then, and only then, can an exchange happen. We must start this process through the "referral" from a trusted friend or advisor to your future prospect. This eliminates the age-old fear-of-being-sold emotion where a prospect is on guard immediately when a conversation begins. Through this referral process, we enter customer relationships with the sole purpose of having a great conversation that's focused around understanding the prospect's needs from their point of view and then, and only then, determine if it is logical to work together. Once that happens, you can embark on an agreement.

Let's recap the ground we've covered so far.

- Telemarketing and cold calling strategies are disruptive and intrusive.

- Prospects and consumers have unlimited access to information and research on every person and every business.

- Most prospecting strategies are highly time-consuming.

Successful sales are a matter of establishing priorities and managing the time around achieving the highest-priority and highest-consequence tasks—and cold calling in today's market is neither efficient nor a high priority.

Here's how we change our selling paradigm. In the same amount of time you previously used to make random calls, you can now, with focused networking and targeted conversations, talk with ten, twenty, thirty, or more prospects who know they need help because they've already done the research. They also know and understand the value of your product and service and are ready to select someone who offers what they need. They are ready to buy.

Once I implemented my Champions' Power Referral Network process, prospects immediately wanted to talk to me because the meeting was established on their terms. Most knew they had a need and needed some help. They were solid candidates ready to hire me and use my services.

After all, how can you possibly claim genuine interest and

concern about a prospect's needs if you have just randomly called them? Selling everything from coaching to selling refrigerators is a personal and emotional issue, and that's true for whatever product or service you represent.

The bottom line is that my prospecting process drastically improves from a random series of events, to referrals from trusted resources for extremely specific opportunities. I improve my time and priority management by 1000% doing more targeted work in less than half of the traditional time spent prospecting.

The second major benefit of the Champions' Power Referral Network is that it allows you to build a huge *personal* sales team of thousands of supporters, for little or no cost.

YOU EASILY SELL YOURSELF!

Most salespeople carry the burden of selling their products and services, selling their talents, selling their product's advantages, and also have all the marketing efforts completely on their shoulders. Successful entrepreneurs the world over will tell you the hardest way to build a business is to try to do it all by yourself.

The Champions' Power Referral Network system builds a huge network of referral "agents" who are constantly recommending you and referring you because they know you, like you, believe in you, and honestly want to help you. I would much rather have 2,000 people thinking about me and recommending me than try to reach that many people all by myself. With this system, you now have that power and it should not cost you more than the price of a cheeseburger.

NOTHING IS EASY

Change is everywhere! Change is necessary! Change and flexibility are required mindsets today for any level of success. Change is happening faster today than ever before and will continue to do so. We cannot stop it. So, absolute acceptance of our current atmosphere is required. If you don't like the way things are . . .tough! There is nothing you can do to stop it, and without change, you will be left behind.

In my *Straight Talk—Thriving In Business* workshop I discuss the 7 LAWS OF BUSINESS SURVIVAL. The first law is:

"If you continue to do business the way you've always done business then YOU WILL be out of business!"

It is essential that we understand our prospects and customers and *earn* their business. The key is to get them to open up and talk to us. *The best way to accomplish that is for your call or appointment to be the result of a suggestion or recommendation from someone that your new prospect knows and trusts.* That is exactly how the Champions' Power Referral Network works.

In Malcom Gladwell's bestselling book, *The Tipping Point,* he defines these people as "connectors" or "the people in a community who know large numbers of people and who are in the habit of making introductions."

Implementing a successful system to find these people is not always easy. It requires discipline. This is the kind of discipline that requires day in, day out, dedication. This is the kind of discipline most salespeople do not take the time to learn and practice.

Champions' ... *"Discipline is the ability to make yourself do what you should do, when you should do it, whether you feel like it or not!"* **Network** ...

™

ELBERT HUBBARD

Top salespeople understand this definition of discipline, are good at applying discipline, and have mastered it. Why? Because *the end result of focused discipline is always success.* No matter what, they always do what they know they need to do and when they need to do it. That doesn't mean they always like to do it or even want to do it, but (and here's the kicker), they do it.

You must learn to challenge everything you once knew or thought you knew about selling. This especially applies to how we think about our customers. One of the greatest changes of the last decade is the way consumers now make their buying decisions. These changes are a direct reflection on how the consumer/prospect/customer have themselves changed. As I've already shared, that's due to technology. People are also now making buying decisions, more than ever before, based on "old-school" emotional reasons. These two shifts have changed how we find prospects and how we position ourselves to be found.

Most traditional media doesn't work anymore. Neither do many of the "fad" social-media platforms. Today, we need to protect our time and not get caught up in the "I'll try it for a while and see if it works" syndrome. We must be absolutely clear about who our perfect client is; how you can help them, based on their needs; where they get their information; and who they know.

KEEPING THE FUNNEL FULL

I have continuously used the Champions' Power Referral Network system for over thirty-five years in one form or another. Through its use, I have become highly successful and feel blessed to have built my entrepreneurial and business coaching career this way. My success has largely been due to the fact that this system has continuously provided qualified prospects for me to meet with—and eventually they ask to buy my services. Because this happens, it allows me to use my time efficiently and effectively, which translates into monetary value.

There is an old adage in the sales game that you must "fill the sales funnel." In this case, the "funnel" is an imaginary receptacle where all your leads and prospects go. In sales, it is always essential that you have a number of prospects that you are working with at the same time. This business truly is a game of numbers, one that creates an equation as to how many prospects you need to get a certain amount of sales. Your sales funnel is the key, but I learned a long time ago that filling the funnel with prospects was not the hard part. The hard part was *keeping the funnel full.* Many salespeople will work hard for a while to fill their funnel, then stop working on their funnel. A month or two will pass and they then find themselves needing more customers, and more sales . . . but their funnel is empty. At this point, there is nothing left to do but take the time-consuming route of starting all over again to refill their sales-prospect funnel. The key is having a system to consistently generate leads that fill your funnel and keep it full. This is what the Champions'

Power Referral Network does.

I understood from the beginning that you *must* sell a customer *before* you can coach them. I also realized that the more clients I sold into my programs, the less time I would have to prospect for new clients. For that reason, the successful implementation of the Champions' Power Referral Network was paramount. And as I believed it would, it worked in a spectacular fashion. Since 2008 I have consistently generated over 150 prospect presentations annually. That's almost four meetings per week, every week! The only way I could generate this many leads was to:

1. Consistently keep my sales-prospect funnel full.

2. Have a powerful and effective system that generates the leads to keep the funnel full.

3. Have a system that consistently creates quality "perfect customer" leads to fill the funnel.

Every year, this system has consistently produced hot leads for me and, more importantly, produced customers at a low cost-per-customer acquisition rate. Note that I did not say cost-per-lead; I said cost-per-customer! Using this system can often eliminate the need for the many forms of expensive marketing we've been told we need. It's just not necessary if you use the Champions' Power Referral Network correctly. In fact, my number one marketing expense in the last decade has been taking my Champions to lunch.

The Champions' Power Referral Network is easily reflected in a similar model that LinkedIn developed that is highly successful. Their model follows this format:

connections>leads>appointments>proposals>sales>new sales funnel

The significant difference between LinkedIn's system and the Champions' Power Referral Network is that users of the Champions' Network don't have to work hard to gain fruitful connections.

Since about 1980, I have never made a cold call. With this system, you simply do not have to make cold calls anymore. Telemarketing is involved, but it's a different style of telemarketing. It is one that focuses on a *non-abrasive, non-threatening, non-intrusive* form of telemarketing that simply works. It works because the traditional "tell 'em and sell 'em" approach is turned upside down by transforming a "pitch" into an enjoyable conversation. That's what prospects and customers want. They want someone who is interested in what they need and want. They want to talk to someone who they think actually cares about their wants and needs. So, give them what they want and sell more in less time.

There are many referral gimmicks and systems and resources available. The Champions' Power Referral Network was developed with a desire to improve time efficiency in the process of finding new clients. Many sales systems and salespeople I knew were cold-calling, networking, going to marketing meetings, and more. That meant they had to do at least three somewhat disparate activities every week. No one wants to do that. This is one of the reasons any salesperson wants to at least give the Champions' Power Referral Network a try.

The system is not rocket science, however, to quote an old and wise street mentor that I was blessed to know in the early 1980s . . .

> **Champions'** ... *"I've seen many educated derelicts and I've concluded that KNOWLEDGE is NOT power . . . APPLICATION of that knowledge is where the real power lies!"* **Network** ...

ALBERT EINSTEIN

To make the Champions' Power Referral Network work, you must implement it completely.

DO NOT SKIP
A SINGLE STEP.

Do NOT just do parts of the system, do it all. Some of it may seem trivial—that's where the secrets are found. There are certain elements of this system that you may be familiar with, but don't let that keep you from implementing this system completely. It's the nuances and slight changes that represent the power of the system. Again, it is a mix of networking strategies and referral strategies rolled into one single system rather than two or three or four specific strategies. It is one system that works and meshes together to form a cohesive no-fail strategy.

Stop and simply take a moment to decide

**"Am I willing to make the commitment to doing this?
If I do, will I be disciplined and exact in its implementation?"**

If your answer is yes on both counts, then it's now time to move forward!

This is going to be fun and profitable. Let's get started!

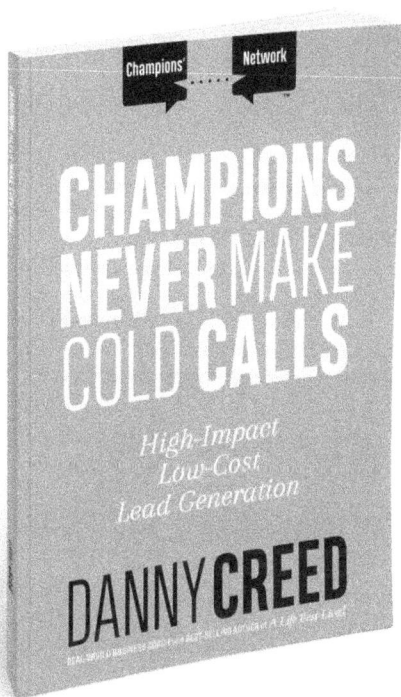

Champions Never Make Cold Calls:
High-Impact, Low-Cost Lead Generation

THE CHAMPIONS' POWER REFERRAL NETWORK™

A Proven Lead Generation, Networking, and Marketing System for Sustainable Sales & Business Growth!

the publishing CIRCLE

• • •

OTHER BOOKS BY DANNY CREED

Champions' Network:
Never Make Another Sales Call

A Life Best Lived

COMING SOON:

Straight Talk on Marketing—
$50,000 Worth of Free Marketing

Straight Talk for Becoming
a Communication Superstar

Straight Talk on Setting and Achieving
Your Goals

Straight Talk—Sales Communication Blueprint

Straight Talk on Mastering the Grind

• • •

Straight **Talk**™

For full information on booking Dan Creed
for personal or professional business coaching,
or to speak at your next meeting,
please visit www.realworldbusinesscoach.com
or call us directly at (602) 697-5949

ABOUT THE AUTHOR

Danny Creed · · ·

MASTER BUSINESS COACH DANNY CREED is an award-winning international master business and executive coach, business consultant, trainer, entrepreneur, best-selling author, and world-class keynote and workshop speaker (www.realworldbusinesscoach. com). He is a recognized expert in sales, management, and start-up business strategic planning. He is also a business turnaround and marketing specialist with a strong emphasis on business development and business growth strategies. Dan is an elite Brian Tracy International Certified Sales Trainer and a Founding Member Trainer and Facilitator of the Brian Tracy Global Corporate Training Courses and the

Sales Success Intensive course. Coach Dan has logged nearly 15,000 business coaching, consulting, and training hours and counting. He has been involved with fourteen successful start-up businesses and over 400 business turnaround challenges. Coach Dan is the unprecedented SIX-time recipient of the FocalPoint International Brian Tracy Award of Sales Excellence.

In December 2011, Coach Dan released his first book, *Bootstrap Business*. The book was a collaborative effort as part of an established and highly successful book series with world-renowned business development experts, Tom Hopkins (*How to Master the Art of Selling*), John Christensen (*FISH!*) and Jack Canfield (*Chicken Soup for the Soul*).

His best-selling second book, *A Life Best Lived; A Story of Life, Death and Second Chances* is available wherever books are sold, or www.businesscoachdan.com/author.

He is also widely published in numerous magazines around the world including *Business Coach Magazine,* serving Eastern Europe, and *Business Venezuela,* the official magazine of the Venezuelan-American Chamber of Commerce.

• • •

To contact Dan for executive one-on-one coaching, workshops, or keynote speaking:

Phone: 602-697-5949
Email: Danny@MrLuckyCoaching.com
Web: www.realworldbusinesscoach.com
LinkedIn: www.linkedin.com/in/businesscoachdan
Newsletter: https://www.fpinl.biz/16/newsletter

* 9 7 8 1 9 4 7 3 9 8 4 6 7 *